How They Lived in
the Lake District

Uniform with this title:
*HOW THEY LIVED IN THE YORKSHIRE DALES

By the same author:
*LAKELAND BIRDS
 LAKELAND MAMMALS (with Peter Delap)
 LAKELAND LAUGHTER
*BEATRIX POTTER (Her Life in the Lake District)
 AFTER YOU, MR WAINWRIGHT
*SACRED PLACES OF THE LAKE DISTRICT
*THE LOST VILLAGE OF MARDALE

*Title still available

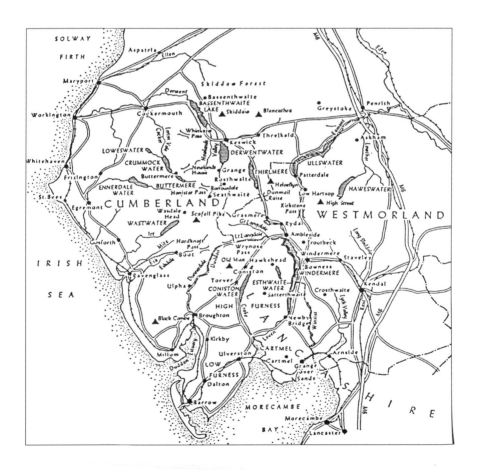

How They Lived in the Lake District

by

W R Mitchell

CASTLEBERG
2002

A **Castleberg** Book.

First published in the United Kingdom in 2002.

Copyright © W R Mitchell 2002.

The moral right of the author has been asserted.

ISBN 1 871064 58 9

Typeset in Slimbach, printed and bound in the United Kingdom by
Lamberts Printers, Station Road, Settle, North Yorkshire, BD24 9AA

Published by Castleberg, 18 Yealand Avenue, Giggleswick, Settle,
North Yorkshire, BD24 0AY.

Contents

Illustrations

Cover picture and line drawings by David Hoyle.
Photographs by W R Mitchell.

Slaters Bridge, Little Langdale

Some Lakeland Sayings

Will Ritson, of Wasdale, said of Wordsworth: "He wor a varra quiet auld man. He'd nea pride aboot him an' varra lile to say."

Of a slow-going son: "Our Frank's just like a cow tail – he's allus ahint."

Of a rogue: "Crooked bi nature is nivver med straight bi eddication."

Of a troubled man: "He snwores at yah end an' belches winnd at t'udder."

6

Lakeland in General

It was spring again. In Lakeland, the raven's young were fledged. The gaunt fells had come alive with the mewing of buzzard, the clacking of wheatear and fluty solo of the ring-ouzel. Herdwick ewes had dropped their diminutive black lambs in meadows that now were as green as any suburban lawn. Soon, the red stags would cast their antlers. Yearling roe, driven from the paternal territory, would wander, footloose and vulnerable to many dangers, looking for sanctuary. Whooper swans had departed in a flurry of white and with musical calls.

A golden eagle appeared suddenly, riding an updraught beside the Cumbrian ridge on which I had decided to have a snack lunch. We stared at each other at a range of no more than 50 yards. An adult eagle, it belonged to the only nesting pair in England. The bird continued to glide, making subtle adjustments to the trim of wings and tail, and became a dark speck in a summer-blue sky.

I envied that eagle its ability to scan vast distances – to take in Lakeland at a glance. Far below the bird's wings were peaks and craggy ranges which, though not particularly large by alpine standards, complement each other to perfection. Green dales radiated from a central mountain dome. Everywhere there was shining water: river, lake and tarn.

This astonishing landscape rises from low surrounds. To the north lies a fertile plain, leading to the sand and saltings of the Solway Firth, with a hint of the blue hills of Scotland beyond. South of the fells are the marshes, sand and mudflats of Morecambe Bay, the channels of which are darkly visible, like the pattern on the back of a leaf. Lakeland is bounded on the west by the Cumbrian Sea and to the east by the broad acres of Edenvale and the billowing Pennines.

Three main zones of visible rock contribute to this variety: the Skiddaw Slates, Borrowdale Volcanics and Silurian rocks. The forms of landscape that are so familiar to us derive from the grinding, rending and plucking of ice. The latest phase of the ice ages was at its maximum about 20,000 years ago, with a final melting only 10,000 years past, which geologically is recent.

Glaciers of local origin tended to follow the old river valleys, which they widened, deepened and rounded into the shape of the letter U; they removed outjutting spurs, carried away screes and other debris, plucked out corries, plastered areas with a mush we call boulder clay, and created the depressions in which lakes formed, their waters held back by moraines.

Over the centuries that have passed, the Cumbrian landform has changed little, but the subsequent vegetation has been greatly modified by man and his domesticated stock. Mesolithic hunters and fishermen, dwelling by a few high tarns, fouled their immediate environment, beyond which stretched forest and marsh. Our hills would be looking bare in the Bronze Age, and the degradation was maintained by the guzzling of goats and sheep and other domesticated animals.

The Romans made a token presence in Lakeland itself by driving a few roads across it, but Britons gave Cumbria its name – land of the Cymry. Norman scribes ignored Cumbria proper when they compiled the Domesday Book; they considered the region to be part of Scotland.

Strangers who first explored Lakeland in the Romantic Age, towards the end of the eighteenth century, did so with some fear and trepidation. They stumbled upon self-centred villages and lonely farms, upon a thinly spread and unsophisticated people, with something of the wonder now reserved for tribes at the headwaters of the Amazon.

Introduction

Over half a century ago, I awoke in a tiny bedroom at a boarding house near Hawkshead, stepped on to cold linoleum and, with a six-inch shiver, scanned frost pictures on the window panes. Washed and dressed, I breakfasted on new-laid eggs, home-cured ham and home-baked bread. It was autumn. Lakeland woods had their Joseph's coat of many colours. The lower slopes of the fells were tinted yellow and orange from the dead fronds of bracken.

As Editor of *Cumbria* magazine, I had become a freeman of the Lake District. Life was still thoroughly local, full of character. It was that friendly, easy-going period when three counties – Cumberland, Westmorland and Lancashire North of the Sands – had wedge-shaped slices of the most astonishing tract of landscape in England. Winter darkness was relieved by the cold light of a full moon and by pin-pricks of light from paraffin lamps at cottages and farms.

In towns and villages were unselfconscious craftsmen blacksmiths, shoe-makers, tailors and tinsmiths. Up to the Great War, there was a Victorian hangover, evidenced by a rigid class structure, with everyone knowing his or her place in society, a strict moral code maintained by church and chapel and a compulsion to work, for the devil had work for idle hands. The tourist season began at Easter and ended in October. Few people walked for pleasure. In Eskdale, just after the 1939-45 war, a farmer shook his head sadly and remarked: "Tourist lot have started coming." He had seen two visitors.

In the Lakeland of long ago, grizzle-grey farmers had little time for owt else but their sheep. Farming was a way of life, not an industry. Villagers made their own fun or just played about, tantalising anyone who came by. "We'd throw hats in for wrestling. On a Sunday afternoon, some of the local farmers would come along to watch us." Worn-out horse-shoes became quoits. "There was a lot of whanging horse-shoes around. Then – to give t'police a bit of a job – we'd play pitch and toss. Nap was a popular card game."

On my Lakeland journeys, in an old Ford car that a Keswick joiner had fitted with new floorboards, well creosoted, I used roads that had scarcely outgrown their old status of country lanes. With cars much less reliable than they are today, every Lakeland journey was an adventure. I crossed Windermere on a coal-burning ferry that had a list to starboard and puffed soot as well as smoke from its wood-bine-type chimney. There was much surreptitious dry-cleaning among the passengers.

When fell-walking, clad in an old raincoat and heavy shoes, I gloried in the grandeur of lonely hills. What would become Grizedale Forest was then merely a green stubble in what had been sheep-country. As I sat down to have a snack meal, I might hear a derisive sneeze from one of the herd-wick sheep whose ancestors must have roamed these parts in pre-history. When you'd taken three pounds of wool off the back of a herdwick yow, it looked a lile thing. It was nonetheless attuned to these rocky, herby hills.

Of course, I heard the claim that the herdwick evolved from sheep washed ashore at St Bees from a storm-battered galleon of the Spanish Armada. (No Spanish ship was wrecked on the Cumberland coast). Another romantic tit-bit associated the herdwick with the colonising Norsemen of over a thousand years ago. (Yet this breed looks like nothing to be found in Iceland or the Western Highlands, where Norsefolk were prominent sheep-breeders).

Josephina Banner, who with her husband Delmar had a fund of happy and curious Lakeland memories, recalled when farmfolk at Eshd'l [Eskdale] Show dined in a barn that had been cleaned out for the occasion. For their lunch of home-cured ham, local lamb and salad, they sat at trestle tables. Music from a concertina and fiddle accompanied the waltzing in a competition on land churned up into mud.

Lakeland buzzed with life. Farmers had large families. There was a reservoir of cheap labour, such as men prepared to work long hours on the farms for little pay and their keep. George Stevens, who started work at the Coniston copper mines, aged eleven, received 4s a week. An adult received a guinea. In the extensive coppice woods, charcoal-burners spent their summers in wigwam-type structures handy to their pitsteads, from which rose plumes of blue-grey smoke. In local villages, the makers of swills wove their baskets from coppice oak boiled and riven into strips. Quarrymen became miners as they hollowed out noble crags for the best slate. Boat-builders at Bowness – craftsmen all – fashioned a variety of craft from rowing boats to the Windermere-type yachts.

Life – simple, stable and quiet – was enacted against a backdrop of shapely mountains. Lakeland had salt-water on three sides. Rain-soaked sheep grazing on the western fells dried off in a "sea-wind". Hoggs [young sheep] had winter holidays on the marshes of Solway and Morecambe Bay. A farmer in tucked-away Hartsop, who did not see much of the sun in winter, told a visitor: "There's gey little bottom land in these parts. Valleys are too narrow, wi' not much flat in t'bottom."

The favourite tale of Wilf Nicholson, who introduced anoraks to Ambleside, was of campers who complained to a farmer that the land allocated to them was too steep. The farmer sympathised with them and remarked: "It's this way, lads. God gave us so much land we had to pile it up in damn great heaps." Wilf told me of some of the simple pleasures of boyhood. He set hundreds of snares, jumping out of bed at daybreak and collecting the dead rabbits before going to school. Many times, the old schoolmistress would comment on his dirty, dishevelled appearance and threaten to stop his rabbiting. It made no difference. Grandfather had taught him how to set snares so he would catch either bucks or does. This depended on the particular type of jump, as revealed by marks on the runs. When he tired of rabbiting, he might tickle sea trout in Winster Beck.

With a high infant mortality, life was cheap. Old Mrs Bowness, in a cottage in Little Langdale, had her funeral wear packed neatly away and told of the days when everyone attending a funeral was handed a piece of *arvel*, a sort of unleavened bread. Farm children grew up close to nature and picked up the "facts of life" from observing the sexual habits of domestic animals. They knew that when a cow uttered a low mooing sound – something like a foghorn, but softer – it was about to deliver a calf.

Dalesfolk were on thin on the ground. Shepherds who bedded down at Black Sail Hut, which became a youth hostel, were ten miles from a road, ten and a-half miles from a shop and nine and a-half miles from the nearest public houses. The nearest family was a good four miles away. A farmer's son at a remote farm grew up seeing "naebody but his fadther and mudther." When a strange man approached the house, "t'lile lad ran in till his mudther and says: 'I'se that fleyt [scared]. There's summat cooming oop to t'door. I don't kna whativver it is – but it's a thing like oor fadther!'"

Two owd-timers who had not seen each other for many years met at Kendal market. The youngest said: "I'se nivver forgitten thee. When *t'Westmorland Gazette* comes, first thing I look for is t'obituaries – to see if thou's deeard." His friend quietly remarked: "I'se bin deeard a lang while. Bud I'm too idle to stiffen!"

Almost everyone walked. A man crossing from Wasdale to Borrowdale, via Sty Head, was overtaken by a thunderplash [heavy storm] and climbed into the large wooden box holding rescue equipment. The latch went over and he was "fastened in". At about eleven o' clock at night, he sensed that someone was sitting on the box. Should he shout? If so, would it alarm the visitor? He risked it. The newcomer, an exhausted walker, had no energy left for flight and released him. The man he had saved now saved him – by taking him down to Seathwaite.

In lean times, dalesfolk went into a state of semi-hibernation. During the Great Slump of the 1920s and 30s, top men on the farms were lucky if they earned £1 a week and lads were "gitting about four or five pund for t'alf year." They worked seven days a week. The effect on stock prices was alarming, with the very best of sheep bringing "six bob a head". Nine fat herdwick ewes made nine shillings a head. A fell farmer who took a cow to Whitehaven returned with £17.

With the inter-war depression acute in 1932, a farm man helped out a friend at Wasdale Head by driving sheep to the sale at the *Lutwidge Arms* at Holmrook. "It was raining. I 'bagged up' fairly well. The rough bag kept the rain from going through. It was rain all the way to Holmrook. I got them sheep sold – ewes for 18s.6d (though some were down to 12s.6d) and lambs for 5s.6d. Rain was bucketing down when I walked back to Wasdale Head. It wasn't a pleasure of a day at all..."

By the mid-1930s, social life was changing rapidly as communications with the outside world improved and machines were becoming commonplace, replacing (on a Lunesdale farm) "a horse and a cart and a sledge and a muck-fork." This farmer did not need to hire labour, having "three gurt lads, big as house-ends and strong as waggin'-hosses." They married, as was the old way, into farming families. One Lakelander said to his son: "Divvent git hod o' thur feckless dris't up [dressed-up] things. Gang thy ways up amang t'fells and find thissen a lass 'at's fit to make a wife on."

Thrift was a necessity, not just a virtue. Ash leaves were gathered at t'back end of t'year and stored in large kists to be fed to the sheep in winter. At West End, in Great Langdale, an old chap mixed ash leaves and hay and carried

this fodder from Mill Beck to a fellside croft. Good hospital-
ity was general – with the odd exception, as when a
Kentmere man delivered a calf to a farm in Longsleddale as
the family was sitting down to dinner. He was offered a chair
and encouraged to talk. He was not invited to join in the
feast. "Owt fresh ower Kentmer?" asked the farmer. "Aye,"
said the visitor, "pig ferrid and brought forth fourteen
piglets, but yon old sow nobbut has thirteen paps." "Why,
mi lad, what's odd piglet bahn to do when its thirsty?" The
visitor observed: "Same as me. I doubt it'll have to sit back!"

The fell pony that had done heavy work about the farm
was usurped by the tractor, especially the "lile grey Fergie"
[Ferguson] which, being low-geared, was well suited to the
steep little fields. In 1921, the Middletons, who had the corn
mill at Lowgill, bought the chassis and engine of a Model T
Ford for £121. It was converted for carrying goods, the "flat"
being made in Kendal and the cab built "among us". Even
so, the horses were retained for the routes on which a motor
vehicle would stall. Yet the converted Model T Ford covered
224,000 miles.

Winter Into Spring

O n starlit nights, snow sparkled and there was absolute
stillness. The high fells might be iced over like
wedding cakes but a low-lying dale remained green.
In a sharp spell, waves lapping against broken ice in the bays
of the lakes created a bell-like tinkling sound.

On January nights, as a courting ritual was unfolding,
foxes communicated with each other through gruff barks and
screams. Amorous dippers warbled while standing on beck-
washed boulders. As snow melted from gullies on the fells,
ravens patched up their twiggy nests. Their young would
hatch out at lambing time, when there was plenty of carrion
in the shape of dead lambs and sheep. Dalesfolk had a
simple faith in the weather lore passed down from father to
son. A green Christmas filled the churchyard. If Candlemas
[February] was fine and clear, expect two winters in one year.

For every assertion there might be found a contradiction.
Many believed that a red sky at night delighted the shepherd
but in the Kendal area "if the sun in red should set; the next
day surely will be wet."

Winter seemed shorter to those who attended social events
like dances or Merry Neets. Women met at Auld Wives'
Hakes, which combined sipping tea with much gossip. Whist
drives were popular and at Christmas the first prize might be
a goose or a leg of mutton.

In mid-March, daffodils, of the small wild variety, bloomed
in wooded areas and along the shoreline of Ullswater, where
they had danced for William and Dorothy Wordsworth.
Spring was tardy in the fell country. The felltops were crusted
with ice long after the official opening date of spring. Snow
lingered in the gills for months on end.

DALEHEAD FARM

Many farmsteads, with their thick walls, small windows, slate porches and roofs, dated from a period that began in the mid-seventeenth century and became known as the Great Re-building. It was a time when, with the Border conflicts over and the wool industry thriving, yeoman farmers with cash in hand were able to replace with something more durable the timber-framed, thatched houses of yore.

At the daleheads, they used the material to hand – slate and volcanic rocks. Beams and permanent features like cupboards were made of heavy oak. Light entered by mullioned windows. On to this simple plan were grafted new ideas as they became popular. In later times, some imposing detached farmhouses were built.

A farmhouse presided over cow-houses, stables and barns, in some of which the "cruck" type of construction, an early style, endured. The so-called spinning galleries on barns were unlikely to have been built for that purpose. They were cramped and cold, being mainly on the north side of buildings. They were probably incorporated to give access, under cover, to an upper floor.

Large families were the rule, so a Lakeland farmhouse was crowded. One family had ten children – twice. A child having died, the number was made up by the birth of another. Sons and daughters who had left school and stayed at home received only the clothes and keep. When the son of a farming family "git wed", the wedding present was £5 – "and that was that!"

A Langdale man who had earned nothing but occasional pocket money after eighteen years of hard work on the family farm, found employment elsewhere. The eldest son in a family might be ill-paid but had the expectation of inheriting the farm on father's death – that is, if mother did not die and father marry again, in which case the property and "brass" passed to the new wife.

A typical farm kitchen had as its focal point a substantial fireplace – hearth and home – that was later produced in cast-iron splendour, flanked by oven and boiler. The necessity for having a regular supply of hot water kept the kitchen fire roaring away summer and winter alike. The hot-water boiler had a tap and water was drawn into a ladin-can.

A fireplace was black-leaded at least once a week and at a Mardale farm a drop of meths was added to the black lead "so it would go further". The farmer at Seathwaite kept a big box of plumbago, from the celebrated local mine, to polish the grates. A steel-topped fender became burnished through frequent applications of polish to which had been added "a bit of ash, sometimes powdered brick." Where the fender lay near the boiler, it was covered by paper in case splashed water spotted or rusted it. In Great Langdale "there'd be a coffee pot on the ledge above the oven."

A fire was set in the farmhouse at Seathwaite using larch-chats and kindling sticks. A horse and cart was driven to Keswick once a month to collect coal from a dealer at the railway station. The everlasting fire ensured that in wet weather, clothes might be dried or aired. They were draped over a winter-hedge, a light free-standing rack, or from a rack that could be raised or lowered, using pulleys that were screwed into the ceiling Hankies in need of drying were laid across the open oven door.

The kitchen was slate-flagged, the flagstones being cleaned using a mixture of carbolic soap or "soft soap" and water. "We got down on hands and knees and scrubbed them." They might be darkened if rubbed with "dolly blue". Flagstones were swept using a besom, the head made of birch-chat or ling [heather] and the comparatively short shaft fashioned from ash. Broom might be used for the head, hence an alternative name. Well-seasoned and kept dry, it would last well, though a damp besom was prone to be attacked by fungus.

The walls of a kitchen were lime-washed at least twice a year, special attention being given to the area around the fireplace "where it got so dirty." A farmer living in Little Langdale took a horse and cart to Coniston station to collect lime and he slakked [immersed] it before use. At this farm, a loft was situated above the kitchen so the ceiling was papered, to avoid flecks of dirt falling on the table.

At Stool End, Great Langdale, "the kitchen had hooks in the ceiling. There were flagged floors – and a stone slopston' [sink] under the far window, with just a cold water tap. Cooking was at an old black range. A table ran practically the length of one side of the kitchen." In Little Langdale, "we had an old laundry table. Father sat at one end in his armchair, which had a rush-seat and chintz cover – and mother was at the other end, sitting on a four-legged coppy [milking stool]. The rest of us sat on forms."

Oil lamps and cannels [candles] provided the illumination. "It's amazing how much heat as well as light a paraffin lamp put out, especially those Aladdins." A special lamp was kept for anyone wishing to go to the earth-closet, across the yard. "They used to clean it out now and again and spread the stuff on the land." The closet was apt to be fly-infested in summer. A visitor who went to use one, returning to complain about the flies, was told to be patient. "At noon, all them flies make for the kitchen." At many a farm, water for the kitchen was "fetched" from t'beck.

The parlour [better room] was used on what one Laker laughingly called State Occasions – weddings, funerals and the like. "Our parlour had a round table with coloured cloth, a rocking chair and 'easy' chairs, each with a antimacasser: a cloth draped across the back of a chair, originally to protect it from anyone who used macasser oil as a hair dressing. There were plenty of ornaments and pictures. A piano was cluttered up with family photographs." The parlour at Wall

End, Great Langdale, had a floor covered by "a crowd of skin mats," from the 1914-18 war, when a good many sheep had been killed and mutton supplied to local households. The cured sheepskins were spread about the house.

A farmhouse bedroom was usually cheerless. The brightest objects were patchwork quilts on the beds. Quilting was a regular winter occupation at a farm in Kentmere where Grannie cut out patterns, squares or diamonds for her quilts. "I was going to school at the time. Every dinnertime, when I came home, there'd be a lile cushion full of needles. I had to thread them because Grannie's eyesight was not very good."

At a farm in Mardale, the bedrooms held iron bedsteads with brass knobs. The sleepers reposed on feather mattresses. The family usually washed in the kitchen but special visitors were provided with a jug of water in a basin. They stood on the dressing table in the bedroom." In Langdale, "my mother-in-law helped me to make a feather bed when I was first married. We got a new 'ticking' and dressed the feathers, cutting the ends off the quills. We also made some feather pillows." In Little Langdale, "our bed had a straw mattress with a feather mattress on top...They used to say you never died in a feather bed – but you do!"

A bedroom at a farm in Little Langdale was open to t'top [it lacked an under-drawing]. "We looked up to slates and rafters." The sleepers were exposed to the worst of the weather. "Before I was married, I was lying on an open bed one winter neet when it began to snow. I could feel t'snow. I pulled t'clothes over me and went to sleep. Next morning, I had to carry one or two swillfuls o' snow downstairs." Auntie Mary escaped the climatic excess, having a large four-poster bed.

WHAT THEY ATE

Food on a Lakeland farm was plain but adequate. On a Lakeland farm, it was "poddish" for breakfast – thick porridge, made in a pan over an open fire, stirred with a stick called a thible and served in basins. Not everyone was thrilled by porridge because "when you'd had a basin full of t'stuff you wanted damn all else. If you had some hard outside work to do, porridge lasted you about an hour, at t'outside, and then you were hungry again. Course, in them days, lads were always hungry!"

At a Borrowdale farm, a bowl of milk was placed on the table. With it was a ladle. "You could have as much milk on your porridge as you wanted." A farm man who had been hired at "a poor spot" was doleful when returning to the farm. He could smell burning porridge. "As soon as t'farmer saw me coming, he stuck a pan of old porridge on the fire and heated it up for supper. I was sick of porridge, bread and cheese. I seemed to get nowt else. For a special treat, they'd let you put a dab of syrup on the porridge. It did liven it up a bit." At Skelwith Bridge, "they set t'pan in t'middle o' table. You could help yourself." At "good spots", a farm lad's breakfast was supplemented by bacon and egg.

At farms where oats were grown, they were milled locally. Farm folk in Great Langdale bought oatmeal from the Windermere grocers. "They sent a chap round for orders, once a month. The stuff was delivered a day or two afterwards. You could buy oatmeal that was medium, fine or pinhead. I liked pinhead the best. It made lovely poddish." Oatmeal was used for another substantial item of food that gave a good stomach something to grind. That item was oatcake (oatmeal, fat and water, with a bit of salt) and a common slimline variant, haverbread which, made on a backstone, was hung up to dry, resembling in its stiff crinkled state a wash-leather.

Much of the food eaten on the farms was of local origin. Old wethers were slaughtered and the flesh dried, just like the hams of a pig. (A former shepherd said he did not like mutton; he'd seen too many wicks in it!). In Little Langdale, it was thought that a three-year-old gelt ewe was the best mutton available. "When I was at home in the bad years [1930s] I used to go round getting orders for wethers [uncastrated sheep]. Then fadder and me would set on and maybe kill two or three sheep in a week. He would stick 'em and I would skin 'em. We cured the legs. It would be getting on for a fortnight afore the meat was ready. We hung it up in the beef-balk [loft] above the fire. Cured mutton had a flavour of its own."

At Birk How, which also stood in Little Langdale, "we dried mutton in that big chimney. We'd choose thick part o' t'shoulder an' t'legs. We put salt and salt petre on 'em and left it for about a week. Sheep's head was used for broth. I loved brains – sheep brains, pig brains. I'd skin 'em, split 'em, take brains out and wash 'em well to make a thick broth. Butchers nearly always gave sheep heads away. If a sheep head was on the small size, we whanged it into t'dog hut."

Pigs were butchered on the farm and the pieces salted before being suspended from hooks in the kitchen to dry. Rabbits not only filled many a belly; they were sometimes so numerous they were sold to dealers from the towns. In the Whicham Valley, "father grew everything – taties, cabbages, carrots, even celery."

In Great Langdale, the mid-morning "bait" consisted of "owt we could catch" – bread and syrup, a sandwich or two or a bit of pasty. For "ten o'clocks" in the field, there might be coffee from a blue enamel can. (The coffee pot was emptied once a week and egg shells were popped in to clean it). Coffee was a supplement to bread and cheese or perhaps "a big lump of gingerbread". Some farmers spurned coffee or even tea and had a pint o' watter after a meal.

Tatie pot – sometimes called "tatie hash" – was everybody's favourite dinner. "You diced some meat and put it in a pan with water and carrots and turnips. This was allowed to boil for a while. Then you put your potatoes on in lumps and they mashed themselves while it was cooking. About half an hour before dinner-time you might put some black puddings on top. Main job was to get it well warmed through."

A hot-pot had the same ingredients as a tatie pot but was drier, being cooked in the oven, not in a pan over the fire. For many years, the hot pot was a feature of social gatherings, such as hunt suppers. It consisted of mutton and potatoes, black pudding, onions and sich like..."

The mid-day meal included pudding – rice, sago or one of the steamed creations such as dumplings made from freshly-picked blackberries. "We'd line a basin with pastry, blackberry and sliced apple, then lay some pastry on top, covering it with a cloth. We steamed it for hours." Dumplings made with currants became the celebrated Spotted Dick, served with a home-made sauce – paste flour made with milk, on which boiling water was poured. A lump of butter and some sugar might be added. Sago was not popular among the children; it resembled frog spawn.

Tea was a modest meal, featuring bread and butter, jam and cheese. There might be home-made cake or pasty, but "not much of that."

BABY BOOM

A native of Borrowdale recalled: "Our two weren't born bi' t'doctor. There was just the nurse. Before that, geyly often, it was just some old lady in the parish." One of the self-taught midwives in Borrowdale was Annie Nuttall. Belle Thirwall, of Bothel, helped women in labour and delivered scores of babies. "Belle arrived a day or so before a bairn was expected. She looked after you for about a fortnight – and did all t'house work as well."

The few doctors, many of them with single-handed practices, undertook heroic journeys to attend to expectant women at outlying farms. The doctor was not usually notified of a pregnancy until three months before the expected birth-date. One day, Dr Kendal of Coniston rode his horse "over to Black Hole and Cockley Beck." Dr Crawford of Keswick journeyed by horse from Keswick to the dalehead at Seathwaite. Dr Matthews, of Kirkby Lonsdale, visited local patients by horse and trap. When the first son of Annie Hobson was due to be born at Hutton Roof, the doctor arrived on a push-bike.

With a birth imminent, someone in the house made rum butter and offered it, spread on bread, to all-comers. Meanwhile, the head of the new-born child had been washed using rum. A dish of rum butter was prepared for a christening. The delicacy consisted of butter, brown sugar, rum and nutmeg. Sometimes, the favoured delicacy was brandy butter. The visitor would press a silver coin into the hand of the child. Before visiting another house, the new mother went to be "churched."

WEEKLY ROUND

Monday was washing day. The operation, performed manually, reduced the women of the house to prostration. In Mardale "we went to the stick shed where the set-pot stood. We got a dozen bucketfuls of water from a pump over the sink in the house. The fire was lit early and we considered we were running late if we didn't have the clothes on the line before 8-30 in summer. We had a rubbing-board, dolly-tub, dolly-legs, a mangle with wooden rollers – and dolly blue, to whiten the clothes. They went through three rinses." In Little Langdale, "our set pot took an hour to warm up. We had plenty of sticks. Coal was ower-dear."

A Borrowdale woman, one of many in the Lake District who washed for other folk, pushed her baby in a pram from Seatoller to Grange so she could continue to do the washing at a house there. The walk, "there and back", was nine miles. In the evening, she left the baby with her husband and walked to another house to do the ironing. "I got a bob a day for washing and t'same for ironing."

Baking day flavoured a farmhouse with wholesome scents. The emissaries of grocers delivered the basic requirements, such as flour, which was in ten-stone bags. Mother might be starting to knead bread as her offspring set off for school at an early hour. Every self-respecting housewife made her own bread, a stone at a time. This was enough for eight loaves. In t'auld days, bread would keep for up to a week in a big pot.

Children at the head of Langdale would bring up the yeast for farmers' wives and at holiday-time the postman obliged. From dale-country ovens came scones and gingerbread, currant and apple pasties, with rhubarb pasty in season.

There'd be a special fruit cake for Christmas – a cake with big raisins and flavoured with rum.

Many farmhouses served "afternoon tea" to visitors. At Seathwaite, something more substantial was on offer – pot of tea, both brown and white bread, scones, jam and rum butter and three sorts of cake. The charge was 1s.4d. Visitors to the *Dungeon Ghyll* hotels, in Great Langdale, sampled lemon cheese, made in winter and kept in large pots, the tops of which were covered with paper that had been soaked in whisky to keep the contents fresh. At the *Dun Bull*, Mardale, ham and eggs were prepared in a huge cast-iron frying pan.

THE MAWSON TOUCH

You could tell when spring had arrived from the show of daffodils, especially in Dora's Field at Rydal and on the shores of Ullswater, where they had been seen and commented upon in prose and verse by the Wordsworths. Azaleas took on a carnival air and blobs of colour enlivened the gloomy groves of rhododendron in the grounds of mansions built for wealthy manufacturers and ship-owners.

A much-respected name in the realm of landscape gardening was Thomas Hayton Mawson. The "Mawson Touch" demonstrated a knack of combining the formal with the informal and included rockeries, lawns and walkways, exotic trees and an assortment of plants that in springtime almost shouted to be noticed.

Thomas Hayton Mawson, youngest son of the landscape gardener, presided over the family nurseries in Lake Road, between Windermere and Bowness. From him I learnt much about Mawson, snr. He was a native of Scorton, between

Preston and Lancaster. His restless family eventually settled in London but in August, 1884, Thomas and his new wife spent their honeymoon in the Lake District. He subsequently put down roots in more than one sense. Foregoing a job with a Surrey firm of nurserymen, he took a long lease of an acre of ground with a cottage and a shop and was joined by his brothers.

As an office boy to one of his uncles, a builder at Lancaster, Thomas had become familiar with the preparation of working drawings and the use and quality of building materials. At the age of twelve, he studied drawing at the Mechanics' Institute under the tutelage of an uncle of Sir Alfred Gilbert, the sculptor. At Windermere, in 1885, neighbours of Mawson Brothers recalled with misgivings others who had attempted to establish a nursery business at the Lake Road site.

It was planned to run a nursery while Thomas developed landscaping. When they were well established, the two parts would separate. This occurred in 1889. Thomas was fond of recalling a time when finances were strained and he received a letter from Mrs Arthur Severn, niece of John Ruskin, of Brantwood. She had recommended him to Mr Bridson, who had just completed Bryerswood at Sawrey and was keen to have a garden laid out. Bridson, understanding the gardener's cash-flow problem, handed Thomas a cheque for £200 and added: "When you want more, let me know!"

Through this contract, Thomas had an introduction to Lady Bective, Captain Bagot of Levens, Colonel Sandys at Graythwaite (an estate adjoining the Bridson property) and Sir Henry Moore of Crook. He was a great Eastern scholar and, wrote Thomas, "the most lovable old man I have ever met." At ninety years of age the old man walked to Windermere, four miles each way, "with a spring and a swing which put to shame many a man half his age."

Mawson's composite style of gardening was to be well seen at Graythwaite Hall. While building a terrace rose garden at Capernwray Hall, Carnforth, for Colonel Marton, he was unexpectedly to render the Colonel a good service. He described his property south of Heysham Docks, then let at a low agricultural rent. Mawson offered to prepare a plan for a new seaport town. He took only three months over this task and, less than a year later, the Midland Railway scheduled the foreshore rights, which were acquired (and paid for) on the basis of its prospective value as building land.

At the close of the nineteenth century, Thomas laid out the gardens of Brockhole for William Gaddum and also travelled to all parts of Britain for private landowners and local authorities. His book, *The Art and Craft of Garden Making*, ran to nine editions and became a textbook on landscape gardening in America. In 1908, he planned the grounds of the Palace of Peace at the Hague and some years later replanned Salonika, the Greek town that had been swept by fire.

INDOMITABLE HERDWICK

I asked a Lakeland parson about his parish routine. Mention was made of his "flock". He smiled and cracked a parsonic joke, saying: "There are white sheep on the hill and black sheep in the dale." The farmers of the central fells were proud of a tough little sheep that greeted strangers to their high domain with a disdainful sneeze. When there was no sun to tak t'chill out of t'grund, sheep had to eat "lile bit's o' briar and bits 'o shoots."

As winter gave way to spring, the sheep, almost all of them of the ancient breed known as herdwick, hunted for new growth. They were well tuned to the volcanic mountains having evolved from the rough crag sheep of early times and yet some of them, in their quest for food, would become cragfast and have to be rescued by men with ropes. "A sheep can brek its neck tummelling from a crag."

In about the tenth century, the Norsemen, who had an economy largely based on sheep, bequeathed a treasury of terms relating to them that are used to this day. Sheep created the bleak Lakeland landscape. Their incessant nibbling ensured there was little or no natural regeneration of timber. Herdwick mutton is less toothsome than it was before the breed was improved to yield bigger joints and softer wool. The skin, cured with salt petre and alum, was made into rugs and mats or into brats [aprons] used at dipping time.

This wiry, goat-like Lakeland sheep took its name from the *herdwyck* or sheep farm, such as that owned by the monks of Furness Abbey. The breed was improved in appearance by breeding to a type in the eighteenth and early nineteenth centuries. Thick-boned, sweet-fleshed, the herdwick sheep was a four-square sheep, with strong white legs that enabled it to stand in a gale without wavering. This tough little breed had a rimy face – hoar-frosted in appearance – and a deep, round body.

The wool, when processed into cloth and left undyed, became the celebrated "hodden grey", as worn by huntsman John Peel. A writer in the first (1920) edition of the herdwick flock book had a preference for dark-coloured sheep, as showing constitution and fitness for mountain life. A farmer rarely found a breuked [dark grey] sheep was "a bad doer."

Fell sheep must gang where t'watter runs – downhill. The herdwicks inhabiting the roof of Lakeland needed to be tough. While still relatively young, the ewes were "drafted" to the low country and for a year or so crossed with mutton-producing strains. The crucial factor on the high fells was the teeth, which wore fast through dealing with such coarse upland fare as heather. A herdwick ewe matured slowly and might not breed until its third year. "It's not the best o' mothers, tending to back away from its lamb. It can be stupid when dug it out of a snowdrift and won't start to eat till it's too late. It lets itself get too low..."

Each herdwick ewe formed a strong attachment to its heaf [natal area] from which it rarely moved and to which it took its offspring. Stocks of sheep were inclined to intermingle at the edges. Richard Warner, a visitor to Lakeland in 1800, was told by a farmer: "Go to the dale on the other side of the mountain and tell So-and so you came from me. I knew him not, but he will receive you kindly, for our sheep mingle upon the mountains." Mingling on the high pastures is not generally part of a herdwick's inclination.

These sheep were weather-wise. In Longsleddale, "it's the odd 'uns that are overblown. Nine times out of ten, the sheep'll come down the fell before they're likely to be caught by snow." The fox was quick to find an overblown sheep. "We had one case where Foxy had scratted-in and chewed the leg of a dead sheep." Tom Fishwick located a snow-bound sheep because he noticed a fox was sitting on the snow, staring fixedly at one spot. Its eyes were focussed on a herdwick that, having used up what bit of grass there was, chewed its wool to keep alive. "We put it in the barn, gave it new milk morning and night for three weeks – and it went on champion."

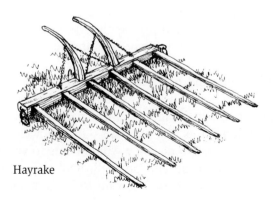

Hayrake

A SHEPHERD'S LIFE

A shepherd going to the fell simply picked up a crook, called to his dogs and strode off. He'd 'appen have a sandwich or two to eat and if he didn't feel hungry would give sandwiches to t'dog. "I had a blow-out [huge meal] at night." A shepherd whose career began at the age of ten when he went to t'fell with his Dad told me: "We'd get back sometime." A Great Langdale man was never lost though "yance I did get out of my latitude in a thick mist. I wanted to get to Red Tarn. I said to missen: 'Thoo's takken t'wrang trod.' So I sat down and git my pipe out and had a smoke. After a while, t'mist split and I was looking reet at Scawfell."

A shepherd at Troutbeck had a four and a quarter mile walk from stable door to t'fell gate. If it was hot weather, he'd set off at between four and six o'clock." A Langdale farmer went round back of t'Pikes three times in a single day – twice while shepherding and once at night to help carry down a visitor who'd fallen and injured himself. A Seathwaite farmer who prided himself on "nivver getting lost on t'fell" told of a lad who did. He slept out all night. "Mist came down and he crept under a stone – him and t'auld dog. They cuddled up together. When mother got up next morning, lad and dog were coming across t'field, large as life!"

A farmer who did not employ a shepherd "bunged" his sheep on to the fell and forget about them until it was time to bring them down for lambing, for spaining [separation of sheep and lambs] or for dipping. "If you were showing sheep, like we used to do, they would come to you because you handled 'em a lot. Out on t'fell, herdwicks were independent and wily; they didn't want to be gathered. They'd skulk away to back of a crag, out o't'rooad. Once they did this, they'd try it again."

Stray sheep picked up in the autumn "gather" were returned to their rightful owners at a Shepherds' Meet, which was also an excuse for drinking and revelry. The Meet held at the *Dun Bull* in Mardale – now a reservoir for thirsty Manchester – took place on the Saturday nearest 20 November. After the strays had been identified, clay-pigeon shooting and hound-trailing were organised. On the day of t'Meet, mine host of the *Dun Bull* cleared the main rooms of everything except the chairs and he distributed beer in buckets. "Folk came for the day. It might be ten days afore t'last of them left."

The event was moved to Bampton, and here Joe Fishwick brought any strays from his farm in Longsleddale. The sheep were driven for six miles over Gatesgarth Pass and, at the head of Mardale, were met by a van provided by Manchester Corporation, who transported the sheep over the last few miles to Bampton.

A Meet which, in the second half of the nineteenth century, took place on the watershed of the High Street range, at 2,000 ft, was moved to the Kirkstone Pass inn, thence to the *Queen's Head*, Troutbeck. Shepherds in Great Langdale and Borrowdale met on the first Saturday in December at the *Old Dungeon Ghyll* one year and the *New* in the following year. At Matterdale, a fox hunt was held in the morning and "a good sing" at night. "A lot of men sang songs and got drunk and forgot to take the sheep home with them. One man took his brother's dog, got drunk – and sold the dog."

Every sheep had its own identification marks. If a dispute occurred, reference was made to the *Shepherd's Guide*, which contained details of the marks of over a thousand Lakeland flocks. Mrs Williamson's flock at Routen had a "cropped near ear, under fold bited far ear, pop on far hook." A sheep belonging to George Kirkby at Beckside was "cropped and under key-bitted near, under-halfed far, three short strokes over back."

For six years, Leslie Grisedale, employed by Harry Blenkhorn, lived and worked as a shepherd on Shap Fell, on the type of landscape known as frog-slother [spawn] and bent [a coarse variety of grass]. He remarked: "I opened the house door – and there was t'fell." His dwelling lay half a mile from the next habitation. His charges, well over five hundred sheep, roamed across five hundred and fifty stubbly acres. All through the year he was busy attending to lambing ewes, wether hoggs, gimmers and geld sheep. Clipping-time was excessively busy. Lambing ewes were the most difficult to clip, for "you have a gey good do if you get an inch rise of new wool."

In one grim winter "we never saw a blade of grass for eight weeks. It was well into March before the hill-ends showed themselves and there was plenty of snow when lambing time came along. Leslie had an anxious time when he was swept down the fell by an avalanche. "The dogs were with me and we were carried down to within five hundred yards of the main road." The snow had broken as they walked round the crag ends. "It was a stroke of luck that I was on the back of it. If I'd been at the front it would have packed me up properly."

A winter occupation for some shepherds was making crooks. A normal crook was from four feet six inches to five feet high. The lamb crook stood at between five and six feet. The wood used was hazel, gathered at the back-end of the year, when "t'sap's oot on it", and seasoned in a well-ventilated spot, such as on the beams in the big barn near to one of the "owl 'oles".

The crook's handle was made of tup horn, of the type collected from dead stock or removed from animals that were finding them troublesome. Not every horn was suitable. The soft pith that formed the core might obtrude, causing unsightly white marks. The crook was roughed out with a rasp and saw before being boiled for between five and ten minutes to soften it. Bending it to the right shape demanded skill and a steady eye. The horn was bent and heated alternately until the shape was right. It was then left to set.

Most of the carving was carried out with a knife. If it was decided to decorate the crook with the head of a fell creature, such as a sheep, fox, hound or terrier, a single wrong move with the knife could spell ruin. The bone was burnt with a hot iron for the brown colouring. Black enamel and white lacquer gave tonal variety.

To get a tight fit between wood and horn, a hole was bored in the horn and the wood carved to fit it tightly. A ferrule made of deer horn covered the joint and gave the crook a neat appearance.

THE HIRINGS

The Hirings were held at Whitsuntide and Martinmas. A farm man was employed for a six months' term at an arranged figure, which was paid at the end of the period worked. He received a shilling when he was hired. "You were then legally fast, same as in t'Army."

The farm man went to the farm with his few possessions, such as a change of clothes, in a tin trunk. He who stood the Hirings was on the look out for a farmer who might offer a comfy home with good food. The lucky lad had a "good spot". A man to be pitied was he who went to a home where the work was akin to slavery and he was not permitted to have his meals with the family. "At some farms, men didn't get enough to eat." A hired man might be provided with a caff [chaff] bed, the material from which the mattress was made having been collected from the ground on threshing days."

Girls as well as boys attended the Hirings. There was practically nothing a girl could do on leaving school but go into "service". Some girls found work at the big houses. Here they came under the demanding attention of housekeepers. A Langdale girl who found a job at White Craggs, Clappersgate, was paid 5s a week. The only break in the working routine was half a day, during which she walked to and from her home. The servants were expected to attend church on Sunday. At Rydal Hall, where the le Fleming family was well disposed towards their staff, a special celebration for them was planned at Christmas. Dancing took place in the servants' hall, to music provided by a local band.

Mostly, girls were employed on the farms "according to size and wit." A broad back was useful in the days when there was much heavy manual work. In Kentmere, "our servants mostly came from Barrow. They'd just left school, at 14 or 15, and were in effect serving their time, learning how to do household work. As they got older, they naturally got better wages. Then they got married."

Annie Hobson, born, bred and married at Hutton Roof, recalled that when she first went into service she was paid 30s for the half year. "You know, it wasn't much but we were a terrible deal happier than what folk are today, when there's one clambering over t'top of another to see who gets the most. I've been a poor woman all mi' life – but I'm out of debt and out o' danger, so I doesn't worry."

At Keswick, "we used to hang about in the *Packhorse* yard or where farm folk were inclined to gather on a Saturday to sell butter or eggs. A chap who didn't get hired went on to Cockermouth.

A Borrowdale lad's first wage, at the age of thirteen, was £4.10s for six months. The largest sum he was paid before joining the Forces in 1914 was £28, by which time "I could do practically anything on the farm." At Keswick, in the late 1930s, you could employ a servant girl for about 3s.6d a week, to be paid at the end of the six months' term.

The plight of the girls who found themselves in the employ of unsympathetic farming families was a matter of local gossip, though most girls were comfortably housed. They were expected to work hard. At Seathwaite, a servant girl, having shaken the mats outside, knelt down to scrub the flagstones in the kitchen and waited until they were dry before replacing the mats. She did that every day, without fail.

A servant girl at High Lodore rose early from her bed and went to a trough in the yard to wash. She was kept busy from the moment her feet touched the bedroom floor. Jane Wilson, the farmer's wife, would shout: "What's ta dewin', Laura?" "I'm fastening me brat [apron]." "Nay – fasten it when thou's coming downstairs and lowse [loose] it when thou's going to bed."

At Penrith, the Hirings were known as "term week" – the prelude to a week's holiday. "You left one place on Saturday and went to the next place on the following Saturday. At Ulverston, a popular place for both lads and lasses, the "lads just stood around on t'side o' t'street. If a farmer thought someone looked like a big lump o' cheap labour, he'd go and see if he could hire him – for as little as possible."

Many girls hired at Ulverston entered new phases of their lives in the Craven district of Yorkshire, where some had the good fortune to have happy marriages with farmers' sons and in due course themselves become farm wives. A servant girl in Mardale was hired direct from home, an arrangement made with the help of the local vicar. At the age of 14 she (and her "canvas trunk") arrived at Chapel Hill. "I went out of Mardale only once during the six months' term. The only money I spent was for the collection at church on Sunday."

During the leanest times, it was enough for a man to have a place to sleep and eat. At Ulverston, in 1930, a time of industrial depression, a man was heard to shout across the street: "Hey, Bill, has ta got hired?" Bill replied: "Aye – has thou?" "Aye. I've got me feet under another chap's table for six months. I'm all right!" That year, "the streets were thick with out-of-work men, many of whom had pinched faces. I found a man who was thin and white and half-starved; he said he would work for nothing rather than miss a place where he could have regular food and keep warm. He had almost starved to death in the previous winter.

"He agreed to come for 50 bob, though I raised his wage a lot later. I gave him a bob to fix the bargain. He was so poor I had to fix him up with coats and boots. By the time he'd been with us for a month, he'd filled out and looked happy. He never went out at nights, unless it was to a local dance, which cost next to nothing. I raised his wage a good bit and he stayed with us for three years."

At Kendal Hirings, scores of men stood around. A farmer would "go amang 'em and ask 'em." A man for hire invariably attached a match stalk or a piece of straw to his cap." A good man could afford to be discriminating. "Instead of a farmer choosin' him, he'd pick t'farmer he wanted to work for!"

A farmer preferred to employ a local lad, from a family he knew well. He could then ignore the Hirings. A Kentmere lad who was employed by his uncle initially received £2 for six months and his pay rose by 10s each term, so that when he left that farm he was earning £6. He uncle did not intend to give him much more so "I told him I was gang to have a change. I knew I could get more at another spot. Old Jack Gilpin, of High Fold, saw me at t'Saturday neet. I'd been down in t'village. He'd heard I was leaving and asked me how much I wanted for t'half year. I said £11. He said: 'Tha can hev it. Start work when you've had your holidays'."

When he had worked for two terms, he considered another change of boss. "I was ploughing one Saturday morning. The old farmers use to yoke up of a Saturday morning to go to Kendal for their week's proven. I was ploughing down bi' t'roadside an' Nathan Gregg and his two sisters came by in their horse an' trap. They stopped. Nathan said: 'I hear thou's leaving.' I said: 'Yes.' He said: 'Will you come to Kentmere Hall and work for us?' I said: 'Aye – if t'money's reet.' Nathan said he'd gie me £16 for t'half year. I said: 'Reet – I'll be there.' And that was that."

A thirteen-year-old Borrowdale lad who began work at Grange Farm at Martinmas arranged for Tommy Graham, the Keswick carter, to transport him and his tin trunk. And so he went forth, wearing an old jacket, a shirt made by his mother – the shirt fastened at the back – corduroy trousers ordered from Mr Huggins, a "bag man" who lived at Ambleside, and clogs made for 10s by Ernie Plaskett of Rosthwaite. The lad's sleeping quarters were over the kitchen. He approached them by a ladder. So constricted was the space beneath the slanting roof he couldn't open his trunk unless he first slid it towards the bed, which was metal-framed. He slept on a feather mattress. Light entered the space through a skylight. In winter, the lad went to bed by candlelight. Little time was spent in the bedroom. He was roused at 6-30 in summer and 7-00 in winter.

HORSES AND FELL PONIES

William Hully, of Orton, one of the great horse-breeders of Lakeland, lived "just on the division between Clydesdales and Shires." William's pride was *Comet*, an entire [uncastrated stallion] that originated on Stainmore and died at the impressive age of thirty." *Comet* weighed 11 cwt and was able to trot a mile in three minutes. "I never had a pony that could gallop as fast as old *Comet* could trot. Each season, this imposing entire served over 160 mares.

The mating round started in May and lasted until the end of June. The man who led the stallion was not allowed to ride except on the last journey home. William Hully said: "Them chaps who travelled entires never got as much money as a cowman; they were nearly always keen on their beer." A man from Whitcham Valley charged £2 for a mating. If it didn't take, only the groom's fee would be met. Farmers living at the head of Great Langdale went to Park Farm, which was visited by a stallion belonging to Moses Edmondson of Ulverston, who employed a man to lead the be-ribboned animal around.

Breaking in a young horse so that it retained "a good mouth" was a job needing patience as well as skill. It might take two or three months. When it was accustomed to having the bit in its mouth, it was introduced to the saddle and tracings. "We used to strap a pair of old trousers, filled with straw, to the back of the horse. We yoked the horse to a log of wood to see if it could pull."

John Kirkpatrick, of Shap, remembered the autumnal horse fairs, held at Brough Hill, for he shod a considerable number of stags, which were unbroken; they gave him a lively time. Occasionally he had to put a twitch in the nose of a stag to keep it quiet. The biggest horse he shod stood at 17 hands. Clydesdales were especially popular. As John explained: "They haven't as much hair on their legs and don't collect the dirt as much as a Shire."

Farmers reckoned you could keep three cows where you kept one horse, which was known to "eat bare". A horse that was given dusty food might become "brokken-winded" and was no further use for work. If haytime was sunny and hot, the horses were roused gey soon. No self-respecting farmer thought of haytime until the third or fourth week in July for sheep were kept in the meadows until late in the season and farmers clipped their sheep in July. The only fertiliser the best land received was bovine muck. In a long dry spell, the hay yield was light.

A Kentmere farmer bred fast trotting horses. His son had the task of riding them for exercise – "half way down t'dale, ower to Ings and up Troutbeck, returning over t'Garburn Pass. In winter, when there was snow or a hard frost, them horses were exercised in a cart. They collected coal at Staveley for t'owd ladies o' Kentmere."

Before the Great War, the postman travelled from Keswick to Seathwaite by horse and trap. "Mother used to send the *Westmorland Gazette* to grandfather each week. As t'postman came up Borrowdale, with his old horse trotting away, you could see him reading t'newspaper."

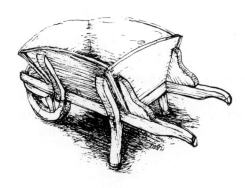

Springtime

Spring was, indeed, tardy on the high fells. Long after it had arrived in the western dales, which opened their mouths to mild sea breezes, encouraging the first flush of new grass, the high fells still had winter in their joints. A fell farmer, gathering sheep, would not have been surprised if a snowflake had settled on his nose.

In the valleys, where lambing-time filled the home fields with stock, the soprano voices of new lambs contrasted with the contralto bleating of the ewes. One also heard the gruff voices of ravens and crows. These birds, dressed in under-taker-black, were, seeking carrion to feed to their young, which clustered in cup-like nests that were lagged with sheep-wool.

Away from the farms, cock ring ouzels, the mountain blackbirds, announced their new arrival from the far south with cold, clear notes that cut through the thin mountain air. On grass-topped fells, skylarks fluttered skywards and warbled. Meadow pipits, descending in a song flight, held their wings and tails stiffly outwards and resembled shuttle-cocks.

To a community that retained a reverence for God, the Easter season filled the churches, from plain little chapels like those at Wythop and Martindale to Ambleside's immense parish church with a steeple high enough to tickle passing clouds. With services over, the people relaxed. Eggs were boiled, decorated and rolled down handy slopes. A trickle of holidaymakers included well-to-do families staying at their favourite hotels for a week or more and day-trippers arriving on cheap railway excursions or travelling in cars with radiators that boiled and bubbled when under stress.

OFF TO SCHOOL

It was not unusual for children living at a remote farm to have a round trip of four or five miles to attend school. A farmer's son in Little Langdale was "never late yance." School was near at hand but each morning he milked two cows and walked a quarter of a mile to feed two young cattle. "Mother did not let me go to school till I'd washed, changed and put on some clean clogs."

Farm children in the Whicham Valley had a walk of nearly four miles to attend school at Thwaite. The children at Wall End, Great Langdale, who were on the register at Chapel Stile school, had a similarly long walk. If the day was really wet, they were kept at home. After school, one of the lads got in the coals while his sister collected some kindling sticks. Then he attended to the hens while sister "did" the ducks. "We had about eight calves to feed. In winter-time we put two great bucketfuls of potatoes out and gave them to the cows. It was during t'war [1914-18] and we couldn't get much cattle cake." Having cut enough taties to re-fill the two buckets, the children had little time for homework or play.

At a village school, children were taught the basic skills – and little else. At Ambleside, "we had 'rithmatic, composition, drawing and reading." Pencils made squeaky noises against the slates that were used for writing. "You cleaned a slate with a cloth and washed it now and again. It had to be thoroughly dry before you could use it again or your writing wouldn't show. We were glad when we began to use paper instead of slate."

Nearly all the children wore clogs. Mr Cullingworth, who had his shop in the Bridge House at Ambleside, was one of the cloggers prepared to make running repairs, such as if a metal caulker became detached. Anyone late for school was caned. "We had to stand in a line just inside the door and – *whack, whack!*" Thomas Fisher, master at Chapel Stile, was "good with a stick... He'd deliver half a dozen strokes at a session." Grace Hetherington, a teacher in Kentmere, was usually kind but caned anyone "for talking". The scholars assembled in the playground and marched into school in orderly ranks. "Somebody played on the piano as we walked in." Anyone who was first with an answer to mental arithmatic got out of school early."

Children living at outlying farms had a snack meal at midday. Those in a Rydal family, attending school at Ambleside, had a partiality for bacon or fried egg sandwiches. "We had a tin of tea or cocoa or whatever we fancied. The teacher set it on an old-fashioned stove to keep it warm." At a rural school near Ambleside, the teacher made "a big pan o' cocoa at dinnertime. We took a few coppers a week to cover the cost." In the Whitcham Valley, "we just had a bit 'o bread and jam and gingerbread, but mother had a really good dinner – tatie hash and stews – when we arrived back home."

LAMBING TIME

Gaps along the "inside" walls were attended to before lambing time and the "outside" walls repaired when the sheep and their lambs were on the fell. At lambing time a valley seemed crowded with life and the voices of the lambs brought responsive urgent calls from their mothers.

The old routine at lambing time was "to git up at dayleet" to walk round the lambing croft. Most lambs were born near the farmstead but "when you gathered in for lambing time, you usually had a few 'white lambs'. They'd bin born on t'fell. If they survived, they were good 'uns. Weaklings died off." Some had their eyes plucked out by daups [carrion crows] attracted by the after-birth and taking every opportunity to attack a defenceless lamb. A fell farmer shot crows, denouncing "them daups" as "wicked owd devils." In Great Langdale, "my father would never let you touch a raven. He said it fed on dead meat and kept t'fells clean."

Lambs could withstand cold as long as it was dry. Ike Wilson, who farmed in Newlands Valley, remembered a heavy fall of snow on April 24, when he was pre-occupied with the lambing flock. "Folk laughed about it and said t'snow would go in five minutes. It stayed and was so deep it came to the top of my legs as I tried to look after t'sheep. There were already forty lambs."

Ike got the sheep under cover the best way he could. "Some had to stay outside and we had fourteen lambs at t'back of the house. One went missing. I looked and better looked without finding it. I got up at half past four the next morning and that lamb was still missing. As I started digging out the yard, I heard a lamb calling. It was just over in the field, its lile head peeping out of a drift. It was aw right, but that spring wasted a lot o'sheep on the fells. They were frozzen to death." Some weakly or ailing lambs were settled in boxes near the kitchen fire and offered cow's milk. A hot poker plunged into it took away the chill. (The "auld drinking fellas" warmed up their ale in the same way).

It was said of a good lamb that it should be cooked twice – yance on t'hill and yance in t'oven. A farmer, going on his rounds of the lambing sheep on a cold, wet morning might comment: "It's a real tickler." He was referring to the method of coaxing a chilled lamb to drink from the ewe. The lamb, having been placed in position to suck from a teat, was tickled at the tail root for stimulation.

A herdwick ewe carried its lamb for twenty of the

grimmest weeks in the year. Then, in April or even in early May, as the first flush of new grass was evident, the ewes parted with their lambs – with tiny black bundles of life. Now, for about a month, a farmer moved restlessly about his fields with lined face and sleep-misted eyes. In cold snaps, he might cat-nap on the horsehair sofa in the kitchen so that he could rise at night and venture forth with a storm lantern, rescuing weakly or chilled lambs.

Most herdwick ewes dropped their lambs without a murmur. Complications included that of a lamb lying the wrong way round or of twins intertwined in mother's body. A ewe's teats might block or the milk flow was affected by a shortage of grass. Then what had appeared to be a lusty lamb lost condition. A sheep that was lambing for the first time was inclined to desert its offspring. A sudden flush of grass culled lambs through what the farmer called "tremblings" or "moss illness".

Orphan lambs and bereaved mothers could be brought together if the birth smell of the lamb was preserved. Normally, following a quick sniff, a ewe kenned its own lamb. Skin a dead lamb, drape the skin over the body of an orphan lamb and the bereaved mother might sniff, then accept it.

Lamb tails were docked, though not too drastically. A farmer liked to see well-covered hind quarters on a lamb. A slice from an ear was the old "law" mark of the Norseman; hence the term "lug". A "smit" mark on the body of a lamb was a further indication of ownership. Tup lambs not required for breeding were castrated using a hot iron. Green salve was applied to deaden the pain.

HORSE POWER

Coaching services gave employment to several hundred men and horses during the summer. Lakeland retained the glamorous four-in-hand, which catered for both mail and passengers into the age of the motor car. As many as eight four-in-hands [horse-drawn coaches] followed a scenic "round" for tourists that was based on Keswick. They traversed Borrowdale, climbed to the slaty heights of Honister, descended into Buttermere and then went over the hause into Newlands Vale.

The livery of the coaches testified that they were owned by well-known hotels. They did not pay the drivers, who were expected to collect a shilling from every passenger. A braking device known as a slipper [wooden wedge slipped under a wheel] was discarded at the bottom of a slope. In the case of Honister, small boys standing beside the road picked up the now-hot slippers and re-attached them to the coaches. Passengers tossed coins to anyone who helped. A nimble lad whose uncle drove one of the coaches made up to five shillings a day.

For an adventurous journey over Kirkstone Pass, the four-in-hand was "slippered" for the descent towards Patterdale. A driver called Willan whose nickname was Lons, took with him a lad who nipped off the coach at the top of the hill and put a slipper under the rear wheel to lock it. The road authority frowned on this primitive form of braking. It left grooves in the road. At other times, the lad sat on the box-seat with Old Willan who, when he felt the need to cut up twist for a smoke, handed him the ribbons [reins]. An Ullswater service operated, twice daily in the season, from the railway station at Penrith to the boat landing at Pooley Bridge.

Dickie Riggs of Windermere operated a celebrated coaching service. Dickie was a Liberal whose photograph was displayed in the homes of Westmorland supporters – until he married a Conservative. Frank Hopkirk, known to his many friends as Hoppy, used to go to Riggs's stables in the evening to help with the harness cleaning and other jobs. At that time, the firm had 150 working horses and others that were "running out".

Eventually, Hoppy worked for Joe Cowperthwaite at the *Rothay Hotel* and, as a coachman, covered the route from Grasmere to Waterhead three times a day. He could recall many of the coach drivers – John Robson, who drove the Grasmere mail; Billy Brockbank, Windermere to Keswick and Jack Hodgson, of Keswick, who was in charge of the Ullswater coach for Roger Bowness, mine host of the *Old England*.

A driver with a humorous disposition was Johnny Greenbank who, when drawing up on the frontage of the *Rothay*, said to his passengers: "You have ten minutes here. When I say ten, I don't mean twenty." By the time he had mentioned local attractions, such as the church and t'old gingerbread shop, the ten minutes had gone and he blew a blast on the coach horn to indicate he was about to move off. At the approach to Dunmail Raise, Greeny – as he was invariably known – called out: "All under seven and over ninety can ride; first-class passengers get out and walk; second-class walk and help to shove; third class, shove."

He, like other drivers, pointed out the rock on the top of Helm Crag which resembled an old lady playing an organ. "Aye," he would add, "if t'wind was in t'right direction, ye wad ha' heard t'music." Greeny was possibly the last man to drive a coach and four from Windermere to Keswick in winter. Only once did he lose his way. After a snowfall, when he could not find the road, he related that "t'first thing I knew, leading hoss hed gitten its foot fast in t'hospital chimney."

Eight or nine horses stabled at the *New Dungeon Ghyll* in Great Langdale maintained a thrice-daily service to Ambleside. The postman travelled to the hotel by horse and trap, leaving them at Wall End and trudging across the fields to Stool End.

John Wilman, who presided over the *Royal* at Kirkby Lonsdale, kept a large stable and owned vehicles of various types. When, in winter, there was not much work for the horses, he loaned them out to Lakeland farmers. Hearing that a farmer in Patterdale was ill-treating one of his horses he made a special journey there to check on the report.

The mail services were maintained through the year but passenger services were reduced at the approach of winter and its consequent lack of tourists. Every autumn saw a great drafting of surplus horses and drivers to the towns and cities of Lancashire and Yorkshire. Other horses used during the tourist season were sold off. Local farmers were keen to buy them, knowing they had been well-fed and groomed.

In September, 1920, the last regular coaching service passed between Windermere and Ullswater via Kirkstone Pass. Not until the 1930s were many of the Lakeland roads given a durable surface.

Langdale Pikes (F S Sanderson)

A Farmer's

Farmhouse at Fellfoot (F S Sanderson)

Haymaking near Fairfield (E Jeffrey)

Lakeland

Dry Stone Walls and Blencathra (F S Sanderson)

ARABLE CROPS

Dalehead farmers might use the plough to grow taties, turnips, oats, even carrots – all being used on the farms. At West End, the farmer made himself a flail to separate chaff and grain. The wooden head of the flail was connected to the shaft by leather, being nailed on each side. A double floor known as a "threshing bit" ensured that the ordinary floor would not be damaged by the whacking of the flail. Grain was subsequently riddled and the chaff was added to food placed in the cow tubs or horse troughs. Nowt was wasted.

When turnips were grown as cattle-feed, they were usually mixed with hay, with husks of semi-ground corn and linseed cake bought from a merchant. "Linseed came in big slabs. I've cracked it many a time. I used to slit a piece in the cake-cracker and twine it. It was damned hard work for a lad. You put linseed in tubs, among turnips and stuff. You soaked chop [chopped straw]. You could alter t'length of t'chopper. Horses needed it short but cows had to have it with a bit o' length; then they could fetch it up to chew." At Sawrey, "we grew oats and turnips for t'cows. We didn't chop turnips up for milkers. They got turnips whole and champed 'em up on their own. We threw two or three in t'boose head and they scooped 'em out themselves."

At Lupton, near Kirkby Lonsdale, John Carr loved ploughing. "We'd set off at eight to half past in the morning and be back for dinner at twelve. At one o'clock we were out in the fields again and work ended for the day at half past five. It was a hard day if you ploughed an acre. You couldn't do it with a stiff ley but ploughing came easier with stubble. My brother ploughed six acres in five days. It warmed both him and the horses up. Mind you, it wasn't hard work when you got used to it. You needed good feet to follow a horse..."

MEN OF SLATE

At Honister, some quarrymen – sparing themselves a long daily walk – ate and slept during the week in rough cabins and went home at the week-end. A man named Gregg never left his work area or his high-level lodgings for four years, storing the sovereigns he earned in small tins. When he had amassed £500, he returned to civilisation, bought himself some decent clothes and a horse and trap and became a spree-drinker. As his money dwindled, he sold the trap and rode on horseback. He subsequently disposed of the gear, then the horse itself. Finally, he was seen walking up by Lodore with a bridle over one arm. Someone offered him 3s.6d for it. He accepted and, after two years "on the spree", returned to work at Honister.

To get the best slate a quarryman had also to be a miner, living a subterranean life, which kept him snug in bad weather though in poor working conditions, the feeble lights being candles stuck to the walls with blobs of clay. When it was customary for several quarrymen to form a team and arrange a "bargain" with the management, they were expected to pay for the gunpowder used for blasting. Half a dozen men needed to produce twenty-four tons of slate for a daily wage of five shillings.

Quarrymen were a tough, uncomplaining bunch of men. At Honister, before an incline railway was installed, a man would load a sled with nearly a quarter of a ton of best slate from excavations high on the face of the crag. Then, deftly controlling the sled, he slithered down the screes for hundreds of feet to transport the slate to the roadside. He then had the toilsome task of walking back up the fell with the sled.

In Borrowdale, Charley Coward got a job as a sledger. He was so pleased he decided to take his new sledge home with him to Langdale so the family might see it. He carried the sledge to the summit of Stake Pass, where he met his father, who declined an invitation to ride home. Charley gave a demonstration by filling the sled with stones and running with it down to Mickleden.

Richard Brownrigg, the fourth generation of his family to work at Honister, nicknamed the pock-marked fell "Egg Shell Mountain" because it had been hollowed out by quarrymen. In his early days, over 130 quarrymen began work at 7-30, after a good hour's walk from their cottage homes in the dale. The working garb was a flannel shirt, a short jacket called a kytel, and "cord" trousers, with hessian wrapped round the bottom of the legs to reduce drag. Clogs were a common form of footwear.

At the quarry face, gunpowder was inserted into a hand-drilled hole using a large hammer and an iron bar called a "jumper". Men working up against the roof of one of the man-made caverns stood on long ladders. They liked to keep the fuse of an explosive short and so it was tickled with a lighted candle set on a pole or even a fishing rod. Blasting was usually undertaken at night, so that when work was resumed in the morning the air was clear of smoke and dust.

I remember when a row of men, known as "rivers", dressed blocks of slate to single-slate thickness, splitting them along the grain. The rough edges of riven slates were trimmed to a standard size by "dressers". A good dresser was capable of handling three tons of slate in a day. Tom Plaskett's skill was such that, when matched against a dressing machine of a type used in Wales, he finished seven minutes in front – with considerably less waste.

High Summer

Wild flowers, a murmuration of insects, the rasping voice of a lovelorn corncrake hidden in a mini-jungle of meadow grass – these testified to the abundance of nature at the peak of the year. The sheep were on the fells, cattle stood hock-deep in fresh grass and, with a little spare time, farmers joined the crowds at the Sports and Shows.

At Endmoor, Gatebeck, Hutton Roof and Lupton, men played knur and spell, a variant of golf, making their own sticks and pum-heads. The balls they used were fashioned from hollin wood. A ball was set on a spring, which was tapped with the pum-head to release it. Up went the ball, hopefully to be whacked on its downward course. "If you missed, you were out."

In hot, sultry weather, fell sheep were troubled by the maggot-fly [bluebottle]. "If a sheep was among t'brackens, the fly laid its eggs on a shoulder. But generally it went for t'back-end. Flies struck at any bit o' dirt. A sheep wi' wicks rubbed and skulked."

A parasite lodging in the head of a sheep led to a condition known as "sturdy". The affected sheep tended to walk in a circle. "We felt all over t'sheep's head for a soft spot. It was generally on t'opposite side to t'way sheep was walking." A hole was burnt through the skull with a heated iron. "You went nice and quietly; you hadn't to press that hard on it." It was then a matter of probing with a fluffy feather for "t'lile bladder that held t'parasite".

After the operation, the luckless sheep was patched up using pitch – to keep out water – and "a lile bit o' cloth." Some sheep got better. Some didn't. In Langdale, "if we had a sheep wi' 'sturdy', and it had any meat on it, we used to eat it."

WORK FOR WALLERS

Symonds wrote of walls dividing the fields in the valley bottom "and then, without warning, rushing up the steep fell sides to meet and converse with the white billowy clouds and the azure blue sky which sometimes condescend to visit the Lakeland hills on a summer's day." Behind the romance lies a story that involves land clearance and the privatisation of much common land.

In the space of a century, from about 1750, the appearance of the Lake District was transformed by a pattern of dry-stone walls. Each wall was really two walls in one, tapering with height, each side bound to the other by small stuff used as filling and topped by a row of capstones, which looked neat and offered protection from the weather.

At Wasdale Head, the flat alluvial landscape was in large part a stonescape, the stones being set in walls or, when surplus to requirements, made into neat piles to clear the land for grazing. Wordsworth compared the pattern of Wasdale walls with "a large piece of lawless patchwork".

A good wall might last a century or more. Where gaps occurred through a shifting of the land or the effect of freeze-thaw conditions in winter, they were "singled up" until there was time for the section to be re-built from the foundations.

Gap-walling was a regular job. In Great Langdale, a farmer said to his small son: "Come on. You can pick lile stones up. You'll allus be of some use." Stones used at Wasdale Head were of the rounded, beck-bottom variety. "If you could wall with Wasdale stone, you could wall anywhere."

Building the walls was a Herculean effort by men who in the early day were paid threepence an hour, a satisfying sum of money. In some cases, horse and sled would be used to move material. The rocks or large pieces of slate could be broken up *in situ*. Norman Nicholson, the Lakeland poet, was to write of walls that walk on stone hooves. He was referring to the many subtle movements that took place from the moment a mortarless wall had been completed.

Some walls strode across the fells, dividing the high grazings but generally the Lakeland fell-tops were devoid of walls, the stocks of sheep keeping to their own ground. Walls did more than fix boundaries. The lee side of a well-made wall was perfect shelter for sheep when rain was being hustled in by a wind full of spite. The rain was intercepted. The passage of air through the wall helped to keep the stock dry.

Because a waller used stone from the handiest source, the walls of Lakeland became a ready guide to local geology. In central Lakeland, walls made of volcanic rocks usually endured. A big red wall above Ennerdale – a wall formed of blocks of granite – hugged the contours in rolling countryside. Beside the Garburn Road, twixt Troutbeck and Kentmere, a length of wall was formed of a large number of thin pieces of fossil rock from a quarry. Near Ambleside and Hawkshead, the field boundaries include lengths made up of interlocking slabs of flagstone.

William Monkhouse, who did much walling for the Naylors in Wasdale, and had known the valley since 1928, told me: "It wad be nice if one o' them auld chaps came back to tell us about t'walls." He mentioned the remote crofts, "lile spots where sheep can find shelter." The Wasdale stones were, as noted, rounded. Said William: "I reckon we should take some sandpaper to 'em so they'll stick." A local farmer who employed a man to gap-wall supplied him with stones. As he passed that way later in the day, the farmer noted that the heap of stones had almost vanished. "You've done well," he said to the waller, who sniffed and replied: "I drooned [drowned] t'lot." He had thrown the useless stones back into the beck.

WINDERMERE FERRY

There was no fuss when the Windermere ferry, a coal-fired boat that had been crossing the lake since 12 January, 1915, touched the shingle after its 500-yard crossing between Westmorland and Lancashire. The voyage, which lasted six minutes, followed a precise course, determined by two cables stretched from shore to shore. It is said that a London lady who knew nothing about the ferry wrote to book a cabin.

A ramp was lowered. A ferryman clad in blue overalls raked the shingle smooth. As passengers and motor vehicles left the boat, others were waiting to board it. Jack Bowman, who had been in charge of the service since 1937, and who had issued me with a ticket, told me that a new ferryboat was in prospect. As I strode towards Ferry House, I looked back to see the trusty craft, with its woodbine-type funnel and the slight list on the side that held the boiler. At holiday time, it had been used by as many as 2,500 passengers a week. During a week in July, 1951, nearly £200 had been taken in tolls.

Joss Hartley, who had just gone off duty, had been driving the ferry for nearly a quarter of a century, shovelling five hundredweight of coal a day to maintain a head of steam. The relief driver, James Sharpe, had worked for the Westmorland Joint Ferry Committee for a decade. At the time of which I write, Leslie Hewkin, an accountant with the Freshwater Biological Association at Ferry House (formerly *Ferry Hotel*) dealt with the ferry's finances. Leslie told me that this ferry had replaced one that was in service for forty years. John Hoggarth, of Far Sawrey, could recall when the ferry was a large boat rowed across the lake by four men. It was capable of transporting horses and carts as well as people.

John was the eldest of eleven children and, starting work at the age of fourteen, he was apprenticed to a building firm at Windermere. Work began at seven o'clock. As the first ferry set sail at that time, he rowed across the lake in a little boat belonging to Samuel, his father, who accompanied him. "On some days we didn't know whether we were in the boat or in the lake. It was nothing fresh in foggy weather for us to be two or three miles off course. I never took much harm – only wet!"

The rowing boat was used until, during the Great War, the start of the working day was changed to eight o'clock. When father retired, he wanted to give the rowing boat to his son, who told him he could keep it. "I'd had enough of that boat by then!" Carriers like Will Knipe and Jackson Atkinson, of Hawkshead, regularly passed through Sawrey on their way to Kendal, setting off early so as to catch the ferry on its first sailing. "They did not return until eight at night. In winter, when candles were lit in the lamps, it was an exciting experience to see the carriers go racing down the road to Hawkshead."

In 1954, I met the man who had driven the ferry on its first run in 1915. John Edward Atkinson of Cunsey, a sprightly eighty-seven, said that for a time there was one cable, not two. This increased the risk of the boat breaking free. The ferry was at first equipped with a large anchor and a lifeboat.

"Cow-jobbers" travelled from farm to farm, buying up beasts to be taken to the mart at Kendal. Then the Windermere ferry resembled Noah's Ark. Joe Abbot, of Crosthwaite, had no sooner got his cows from Lancashire to the Westmorland shore than they split up into two groups. One group decided to swim back. Fortunately, a man in a punt manoeuvred it to the low side of the ferry and the two craft slowly crossed with the cattle bunched between them.

Having a ferryboat with a ramp at each side could be

confusing to passengers in a hurry. A man who sprinted along the Lancashire shore and took a flying leap on to the boat as it was several yards from shore, gasped: "That was a near thing." Said the ferryman: "Not really. We're coming in."

John remembered the gracious days when wealthy families had their own craft on Windermere. Throttling back to thwart the owner of a launch who habitually drove it near the ferry, John had the satisfaction to seeing it hanging on the cables. He drove Sir Edward Holt's steam launch and, later, the electric launch owned by Ben Townson of Storrs. The vessel owned by Mr Kirk, of Samuel Kirk, the Leeds dyers, had a stock of champagne and cigars on board. John Atkinson, the driver, was not invited to partake but he retained kind thoughts of Mr Kirk who, after a trip on the lake, gave him a golden tip – a sovereign or half sovereign.

COLLIES ON TRIAL

The Border collie, a favourite with Lakeland sheep farmers, had been bred on each side of the border for many years. A hill collie must have a good wide run on the fell and must not be afraid to use itself. In doing this, it must give the sheep plenty of room. Joseph Ralph, who lived in St John's Vale, trained dogs, giving each dog one of the short, sharp names that might be heard at a distance outdoors. These included Tuss, Mac, Bright, Jack and Kip.

When training his dogs, Joseph did not keep his youngsters shut up in case they spoiled. "Let them play about," was his advice. "Let a young dog go with you whenever possible. Then it will develop mentally and it's half broken in before it need bother about sheep. If you keep a dog shut up in a kennel, it's like shutting up a small boy in a dungeon."

Joseph sometimes took three or four with him when gathering sheep. He did not want any one dog to be overworked. "If you have one dog running to the right when you are gathering a breast and then there's a job to do on the left, you've got to run the dog over a lot of dead ground – maybe half a mile – before it gets a start. With two dogs, time and effort are saved." He reckoned that a dog that was always on the move might cover fifty miles of fell in the day.

Not all sheepdogs were collies. At Wasdale Head, some curs – when not gathering sheep – went off fox-hunting on their own. Many farmers and shepherds trained their own sheepdogs, though "a dog trains itself as long as you keep on top of it. I had one that showed interest when it was six months old. Another dog was two years old before it did a stroke." Whistled commands were unemotional. "I used to whistle with my fingers till these [false teeth] spoiled it." Some sheepdogs were rough-haired, others clean and smooth-haired. A fell farmer liked a dog that barked when asked to bark. A good dog worked for one man only. "I'd one. I let t'pup out with it."

Some people consider that sheep are unintelligent. Joseph Ralph's experience was that they are very clever. "Sheep will notice any weakness in the dog." Sheep can be wild. "The dog has to have that uncanny ability of being able to quieten them – putting them at their ease."

One of the first sheepdog trials I attended took place under a cloudless August sky. The venue was a field between Caldbeck and Hesket Newmarket. There was a thoroughly rural setting – field upon field, with a backdrop of the rolling fell-country to the north of Skiddaw. An early start was planned. At 8 a.m., dew still lay on the showfield. By noon, even the worms would be panting. No one complained of the weather, doubtless recalling the wet and windy conditions of other occasions, when both man and his collie dog felt miserable. It seems there is a difference in whistle-carrying power between dry and wet ground. "Sound slows up a bit ower bogs." The whistle is a clear, no-nonsense command that, in good weather, might be heard at a distance of one and a-half miles.

Some collies excel at trials but are not suited to work among the brackens on high fell farms. Conversely, some fell-type dogs lack the sophistication necessary for star performances before a crowd. One of the worst crimes in a sheepdog trial is for a dog to bark. "There's no law again it," said an enthusiast, "but let's put it this way – barking doesn't help a dog's chances."

I watched as trialists booked their names on arrival – prepared to take their turns according to the list. I questioned a man who soon lost patience in explaining the elements of a pastime he had known since his childhood. "All tha needs to knaw," I was told, "is that the dog moves off on an outrun. If it's taking sheep away, it's on a *drive* and when it brings the sheep back, it's a *fetch*."

A competitor took up his position at a post near the judge's stand, a quite ordinary trailer. The man sent his dog on the outrun, leading to where three bemused sheep were standing. As the dog approached, the sheep bunched and moved forward with a rather haughty gait, holding their heads well up. They must be kept moving, without becoming excited. Trotting was one thing. Sheep at the run were "chucking away points".

The sheep came towards us, on what should be – but is not always – a straight line. "He's git yon sheep ditherin'," said one of the spectators. The animals were driven through an eighteen feet gap between two hurdles. The dog zig-zagged, then flopped when all seemed to be going well. The trialist whistled – low, crooning whistles that became sharp and highly-pitched when things were not going right. Three flighty sheep were driven behind him and away to a gap in some more hurdles. A tight turn followed, then another sortie between the first hurdles.

During the attempt to pen the sheep – the ultimate challenge to man and dog – you could have heard a Cumberland pasty drop. The competitor had the rope from the gate to the pen in one hand, crook in the other hand. His arms were outstretched. His nerves were as tense as watch-springs. The dog, half-hidden by grass, stared at the sheep, which stood, only their heads moving, wildly, as though they were responding to that deep fear that centuries of association with mint sauce had bred in them.

The man stood, trying not to appear exasperated. The dog inched forward, hoping to trigger off some response in the sheep. There was an anti-climax. A shrill note from a metal whistle reminded us that this was a time-trial. Six minutes had elapsed. Time was up.

TAKKIN' 'OD

Hod, hype, hank, clicks – these are words of action used in Cumberland and Westmorland style wrestling, said to date back to the day when Jacob wrestled with the Angel. It was probably a popular sport in Norse times. For centuries, next-to-nothing was written about it. There was no recognised text book but much was written about wrestling celebrities.

When Ike Wilson, of Newlands, was a teenager, he joined a score of other lads who were organising wrestling bouts. "On a sunny evening, the lads threw caps into a heap. A chap sat on the hats. Two hats at a time were drawn out of the heap. The owners of those hats had to wrestle. The losers put their caps on their heads. It went on till there was only one lad with a bare head. He was considered to be the best wrestler."

From May until October, fans gathered at the agricultural shows and sports days to see lads "tak 'od". Toughness and science combined in a sport that demanded more technique than brute strength. Lads engaged in farm work or forestry had toughness. On special days, the competitors wore traditional garb of silk vest and slips, with coloured trunks, often elaborately embroidered, and socks.

A contest was judged on the basis of three falls and under the supervision of two umpires and a referee. Two wrestlers entered the ring and shook hands. They gripped each other round the back. The bout began when fair holds had been taken and the referee shouted "hods". A good "hod" was vital and the wrestlers gripped each other as low down the back as possible. Both bent their bodies so they were almost horizontal and their legs were kept wide apart for stability. A man would lose the fall if he broke his hold.

A fall might come in ten seconds – or ten minutes. Special names for the standard throws included inside and outside hype, the right and left back-heel, twist off the breast, swinging hype, right and left leg hank, full buttock, half buttock and cross buttock. Skill and experience soon told.

The first wrestler to touch the ground with any part of his body other than his feet was declared the loser. Sometimes the outcome of a bout was in doubt, both men falling side by side in what was called a "dog" fall; they wrestled again to determine the winner.

BUTTER AND CHEESE

Scarcely any milk left the farm as milk. It was converted into butter or, much less commonly, into cheese. Milk was poured into bowls that were left on a slab of stone in the milk-house for "three meals", when the cream was carefully removed, the remaining [blue] milk being fed to the young stock. The quality of butter varied subtly from farm to farm. Cheese made with blue milk had a crust as hard as paving-stones. One farmer put many a lot in his pocket and chewed it between meals.

A Rydal farmer's wife poured her milk into distinctive large bowls – brown outside, yellowish inside – and, when the cream was at the top, "she held a bowl up and loosed the edges of the cream with a finger, then blew it off into a cream pot." A farmer in Kentmere had some milk leads, metal containers, with sloping upper sides and a plughole through which the blue milk ran off. The kitchen where t'cream pot stood faced north so there was no direct sunlight. "Everything was cold and clean."

At Bootle, the separation of the cream was affected by putting the milk in "bowls wi' spouts on. You poured t'milk through t'spout and the cream stopped behind." Eventually "We carried t'milk into t'house, siled it and separated it wi' one of them proper separators that you twined [turned]."

Churning day was vividly recalled. It could be protracted in summer. "At my uncle's farm, Monday morning was set aside for churning. He had yan o' those gurt, beggering things that med sixty pund o' butter at a time. Twining the thing was murder! In hot weather you'd be twining for over an hour and a half." A farm in St John's Vale supplied the *Royal Oak* at Keswick and several other busy hostelries. Butter production peaked at ninety-five pounds a week.

"The week we totalled 95 pund was in summer and the weather was very hot. We got up at night and did half of it; then we did the other half early next morning before t'sun had got up."

Scotch Hands [small wooden grooved bats] were used to shape the butter into saleable portions. A wooden bowl was used, the butter being beaten against the side to get moisture out – you might hear it go *plop-plop, plop-plop* – and to mix into it some salt. A skilful person might adorn an oblong block of butter with a pattern, using the edge of one of the Scotch Hands. "Round pounds" of butter were adorned with the imprint of some familiar object like a thistle, a rose or even a cow.

Butter was sold locally, being collected by a "badger" or delivered to a grocer, who deduced the value of the butter from the farmer's monthly account for provisions. Kentmere farmers delivered butter to the Threlfall brothers of Staveley. A butter-producer in the Whicham Valley took his output to Millom Co-op. The farmer at Seathwaite delivered butter by horse and trap to Bowdens, in Lake Road, Keswick. Several large-scale grocers in Penrith collected butter, cheese and eggs from the farms.

At Crook, two days of each week at one farm were devoted to making cream cheese. Cream was separated from the milk and salt added before it was hung in a close calico cloth for the whey to drip away, being then pressed solid. The cheese was wrapped in a small piece of muslin. A cheese that tipped the scale at twelve ounces cost 1s.6d. The more popular size, weighing six ounces, was retailed at eightpence. In Mardale, a zinc bath, kept in the "middle scullery" of the farm, was used for converting the surplus milk into cheese.

A girl hired at Ulverston developed a strong dislike of farmhouse cheese when "t'missus med big round 'uns and got me to taste 'em in case there wasn't enough salt. I didn't touch cheese after leaving that farm."

Above: Butter-making at Gatesgarth *(S H Cole)*.
Below: Fireside relaxation at Seathwaite, head of Borrowdale.

A WALL MADE OF SLATE
The two men are setting up a frame for a new wall
east of Coniston Water.

Above: Peggy Crosland, of Bowness, with one of her trusty fell
ponies decked with two sacks of fodder.
Below: Shorthorn cow, a favourite with old-time Lakeland farmers.

Lakeland architecture. *Above:* Lakeside, Windermere.
Below: Wythop Church, Thirlmere.

Two lads, in traditional garb, wrestling in the Cumberland and
Westmorland style at Grasmere Sports.

A SHORN HERDWICK
Clipping a sheep with hand-shears in the yard of a farm at the head
of Buttermere.

Horses and Pony. *Above:* A line-up of working horses in the
Gunpowder Parade at Chapel Stile, Great Langdale.
Below: A fell pony of a type that was widely used.

Spectators at a sheepdog trial. Whistling is an unemotional way of directing dogs when gathering sheep on the fells.

SICKNESS AND HEALTH

When Ned Tyson, of Dale Head, met Old Dr Johnson, he was asked: "How are you?" Ned replied: "I'm not telling thee 'cos t'last time thou axed me how I was, you sent me a bill for seven and a tanner." Linseed poultices were used for "drawing things". Other poultices were made of bread. "Soft brown bread's the best". When a man had a boil on his neck, his wife slapped on it a poultice formed of brown sugar and soap. "He nivver had any boils after that."

In t'owd days, each farmer must be his own vet. At Seathwaite: "An old man came round and took the loose teeth out of the heifers." Medicines for stock were kept in a dry spot, such as the "spice cupboard" by the kitchen fire. Among the items available if a cow was ailing were castor oil, brimstone and treacle. "Treacle was a good medicine. We got it at t'grocer's in a stone jar, fourteen pound at a time. If a cow had a stoppage, we'd give it beer and treacle or castor oil." At some farms, medicines were administered from a cow's horn.

A Shorthorn cow was relatively healthy and the small size of the average milk herd enabled the farmer to spot ailments in good time. His response might be surprising. "I yance made a mustard plaster for pneumonia – aye, brown paper covered with a dollop of hot mustard. I just clapped it on t'cow near its lungs. Mind, t'cure took a long time to work but there was never a cow lost." Another farmer who used this remedy used "soft" mustard and slapped the poultice round its ribs. "Then I'd get a bottle o' summat for it to have a drink. By gum, it got better."

T'owd chaps used to talk about a cow getting "worm in t'tail", which might be cured by sticking a knife through the thinnest part. They also mentioned a cure for goodness knows what that involved lacerating the dewlap of a cow to admit a tape on which mustard was placed. The tape was periodically moved round.

Abortion was feared: a whole herd could be affected in short time. At Sawrey, "we never had anything o' t'sooart till we took over this farm on our own. Then it started right away. Abortion. Ivvery cow did it, bar one, and that was a white one. We hadn't much money and were owing a bit, so t'abortion job nearly finished us off." In desperation, a farmer might tether a goat in the byre or hang some Epsom salts above the door. It was akin to black magic. If it worked, it was tried again, even though the complaint was unlikely to affect the cattle for a second time.

No one hears about John's Disease now. "It seemed to go when folk started to put a lot o' lime on the land." Affected cattle "scoured and wasted away".

AT THE SMIDDY

A blacksmith's life demanded hard work for little return. It was "blood for money". Yet two blacksmiths who lived in Old Westmorland worked at the smiddy for over sixty years and were well over ninety years of age when they died. They were Jonty Wilson of Kirkby Lonsdale and Joe Tallon who lived at Lupton.

Joe began work at the age of eleven and was paid ten shillings a week, which then was considered a good wage. It was nearly all horse-work. Some of the horses brought for shoeing were high-spirited. George Airey, of Spital Farm, arrived with an animal that nearly kicked the smiddy to bits. A local man commented; "By gum, Joe, I wouldn't shoe that horse if they gave me all Lupton."

Eventually, a pulley was driven into a beam and the horse was hoisted off the ground by its fetlocks. Even George found it too much for him. He sold it to the people at Gatebeck Gunpowder Factory, where it was set to work hauling railway wagons down the track to Milnthorpe station. The horse's spirit remained unbroken.

The blacksmith of yore removed "wolf" teeth from the mouths of horses using a hammer and chisel, which was "rather awk'ard for a lile chap sich as me." He put rings in the noses of pigs and bulls. Joe made one of the pincers used by Albion Ducket, whose speciality was pulling out the ailing teeth of cows.

In ploughing country, Joe worked long hours. He was frequently at his workplace, sharpening plough-irons, at nine o'clock at night. In those days, when ploughs were wheel-less, the irons must be trimmed regularly. If you were working sharp land, as at Barbon, the irons must be attended to almost every other day. "You hadn't time to get owt to eat."

The "Gondola" on Coniston Water

CLIPPING TIME

About a fortnight before clipping-time, "we dammed t'beck, penned t'sheep, then chucked 'em in." At the wash-dub, fleeces were cleaned and the wool helped to "rise". Near Bootle, "we washed yance or twice. You were supposed to get more per pound for your wool. We never did. Anything you gained by washing you lost in weight." Sheep-washing "faded because of t'maggots. Blowfly struck sheep afore they were dry."

Clipping took place between late June and t'latter part of July. A ewe with a lamb was not in as forward a condition as other sheep. If the wool was removed too soon, the animal was starved [chilled]. The lamb might be starved with the loss of mother's milk supply. A herdwick had "roughish wool" and was "hard to clip".

For what was known as a boon-clip, neighbours and friends gathered at the farms in turn to shear the sheep. "Clipping time was never the same after t'first war." Hitherto sheep by the hundred and people by the score gathered at a farm on a special day to harvest the wool. At Chapel Farm, Borrowdale, "there'd be six clipping, three catching, two smitting [applying fresh sheep marks]. In Mardale, "there'd be three or four clippers, with a couple o' lads catching and an old man folding fleeces."

At Gillerthwaite in Ennerdale between 2,000 and 3,000 sheep were clipped by over twenty shearers. They sat in a circle, being supplied with sheep by a small army of helpers. If anyone wanted a sheep at Gillerthwaite, they shouted "Billy Ben", after an old-time shepherd of that name.

The farmer at Seathwaite, Borrowdale, who had well over a thousand sheep, clipped the hoggs first, then tackled the shearlings. The last to be shorn were the ewes. "It went on for maybe a fortnight, even three weeks in some years."

In the Langdales, boon-clips occurred at Fell Foot, Birk Howe and Base Brown. "The men gathered afore dayleet. As first leet came, they were ready on t'tops to gather sheep. For the clipping, they had two or three big strong lads catching sheep. We children took round salve and bandages in case a sheep was cut." Yet more children gathered up the wool. With clipping done, lambs that had been separated from their mothers were re-united in a flurry of movement and a cacophony of sound. For a time chaos reigned. Mother might recognise her own youngster by the smell but during clipping her appearance had changed so much that for a time recognition might not be mutual.

"There were always a lot of short ends that had been clipped off. If they were clean, they were picked up and put in a heap. At our farm, fleeces were thrown in a heap on the barn floor. Folding 'em was a wet-day job." Ike Morris, from Pickles, the wool merchants of Kendal, was a dab-hand at folding fleeces. "He often turned up at Middle Fell and it was good to watch him folding them up.

There was a knack in t'fleecing business. In t'auld days, they put handfuls of small clippings into a fleece before wrapping it." Wool was wrapped up in big sheets. A horse and cart transported the wool from Seathwaite to Keswick. One year, when wool was bringing twopence a pound, the Seathwaite farmer would not sell. With the outbreak of the Great War there was a considerable demand for wool and the price greatly improved. Contrariwise, as they used to say, Isaac Thompson, of West Head, Thirlmere, kept his wool-clip for three years because it was bringing only thruppence a pound. Eventually he had to sell it – for tuppence.

Among the refreshments at Wall End, Langdale, were brandy snaps. "When I was a girl, I'd go across to the farm when they were getting ready for their clipping. In the front kitchen they had sticks spread out all over. When they'd baked the brandy snaps, they put them round the sticks to make them curl." At clipping-time, women did the catering, bringing round the beer jugs and providing tea, with sandwiches made of home-cured ham. When the clipping ended, at about six o' clock, the men, stripped to their waists, washed in shallow tubs. Everyone then sat down to a hot-pot.

The Clipping Party took place in an outbuilding and, for dancing, the wooden floor was smeared with candle fat. "I was never much of a dancer, but I used to enjoy listening to my old boss, Noble Gregg, as he played the melodeon... Occasionally t'beer can 'ud go round. At one 'do' a chap got tipsy. They put him through t'trap door they used for serving fodder to t'stock. He finished up in t'coo-spot down below." In Langdale, "one of my uncles played his melodeon. At about four o'clock in the morning, he'd gently play *Now the Day is Over*. It was time for everyone to gang home!"

The Great War killed the boon-clip. "There were hardly any active men left. Those that remained did the best they could..." At Kentmere Hall, a manufacturer of clipping machines demonstrated them in the yard on a day when the usual helpers, sitting on creels and using hand-shears, went about the work in the traditional way. They were interested and amused, each man clipping two sheep while the machine did one.

CHARCOAL-BURNERS

In Arthur Ransome's *Swallows and Amazons*, the children met some charcoal-burners in the woods. A wigwam-like structure was the base from which they attended a smoking heap of wood covered by soil. The "pitstead" must smoulder and not be allowed to burst into flame. Such activity took place in the coppice woods, and especially around Backbarrow on the Leven, until the early 1920s.

My old friend Jack Allonby, who lived at Spark Bridge, was consulted when the charcoal-burn was needed during the filming of *Swallows and Amazons*. Coppice woods, a subtle harmony of young trees of various species, covered a large area of Southern Lakeland. A tract was clear-felled every fifteen years or so, the season beginning in November and lasting through the winter until early April, beyond which the following year's growth would be ruined.

John Major, a woodman all his working life, whose home was a cottage mid-way between Ferry House and Lakeside, and who retired from woodland work in 1947, had heard of t'auld days when coppice woods were sold by auction. The venue of the Graythwaite Hall sale was Eelhouse, on the top road. The woods were numbered and named on the maps, which also gave the number of acres. So many lots were offered annually. A coppice wood belonging to Low Graythwaite sold at Lakeside for £22 an acre.

Thin stuff off the birch, known as *chats*, was made into besoms for use in gardens or foundry-besoms, which were consigned to industrial Glasgow in batches of 500 dozen. Other woodland crafts were the making of swills [agricultural baskets], hoops for gunpowder barrels and fenders for ships. Birch, ash or sycamore with a diameter of at least $2^{1}/_{2}$ inches was classified as "bobbin wood", to be converted into reels for the textile industry.

Straight ash and oak were consigned to the Potteries for the making of crates. May to July was the season for oak bark-peeling to meet a steady demand from the leather-tanners, the peeling process being known as *rhining*. By July, the sap stopped running. Oak bark was stacked to dry and in August was taken under cover. Subsequently, it was chopped into small pieces and packed for despatch to the tanneries.

The men who felled the trees and cut the wood into handy lengths for charcoal-burning were paid according to the number of bags in a pit, usually about three and a half dozen. If six dozen bags were used, the pit was reckoned to be a large one. Men engaged in such piece work had to give the long count [six score to the hundred]. After the Great War, the "short 100" was introduced.

As a woodman living at Bandrake Head, and earning 25s shillings a week, Tyson Allonby recalled carrying an axe weighing up to seven pounds to remote spots and to areas that were steep, rocky and treacherous. When he slipped on to his axe while working at Dale Park, the wound needed three stitches. When he was "charcoaling" and living in the woods, his mother visited him by pony and trap, bringing him home-baked potato pies.

Charcoal production was for the furnace at Backbarrow, established early in the eighteenth century, and later for the gunpowder factories, several of which were to be found in the Southern Lakes. The "pitstead" at which the burning took place was originally a pit and the name persisted when the pyre was set up on level ground. A pitstead consisted of about fifteen tons of wood that would be covered by six tons of soil – three tons for keeping the fire in and three to be used later when it was necessary to put it out.

The process began when billets, stakes with a length of from 2 ft to 3 ft, were arranged round a stout central stake. As Jack said, you needed "strong stuff at the heart and the small stuff outside". The wood was allowed to season. The combustion season began about the middle of August when a ladder was reared against the pitstead and the central stake removed, to be replaced by red embers poured in from a shovel. Thus did the burn begin in the centre and worked its way slowly outwards in a circle. If the firing took place about 9-30 a.m., combustion would have ended about two or three o'clock on the following afternoon.

The "charcoalers" must be in constant attendance, covering the pile with soil and erecting windproof hurdles to control the combustion. Hot-spots likely to burst into flame were doused with water from flat tin dishes known as *sayes*. Sifted earth was deftly applied using long-shafted shovels. When combustion was complete, the fire was smothered, the pile raked down and left to cool. The charcoal was transported in sacks to where it was required.

The "earth cabin" that provided on-site accommodation consided of a low circular wall, with a hearth and a gap for entry. On it was made a conical structure, using local wood. The men, who neither washed nor shaved, became black from the smoke and grime in a "burning" season extending until the end of October and, occasionally, into November. Charcoal was put in sacks for transportation. The income of the charcoal-burners was based on the number of tons produced.

IN THE HAYFIELD

During the third or fourth week of July, teams of men felled the meadow grass using the straight-shafted ley [scythe], which had a blade up to six feet long. An Ambleside man who, as a lad, had been the fourteenth scytheman going down a meadow, remembered when a storm left a field in Little Langdale in a terrible state. Said the farmer to the lad, who had just left school: "Thee an' me's gang to mow it." It was a task the lad would never forget. "Talk aboot punishment! Yon field was nearly six-acres. After mowing it, I was that sore round ribs for two or three days I hardly dare breath. Then I was all-reet."

Quarrymen in Little Langdale were handy with the ley. In Kentmere, "they'd given up mowing by scythe when I was a nipper, just afore t'first world war, but it still went on at some of t'high fell farms." A Borrowdale farmer was loyal to his scythe after the coming of the first machines. When horse-drawn contraptions were clattering round the meadows, he was on his own, mowing hill-ends and dyke-backs.

The old-fashioned way of giving the scythe-blade a "new edge" was to sharpen it with a strickle. This was a piece of wood with flat sides and a shaped handle that was normally attached to the scythe helped to balance it. The strickle was pitted with holes, smeared with pitch or bacon fat, then dusted with fine hard sand – the sort of sand one might find at the edge of an upland tarn. This gave it an abrasive surface.

Farmer Coates, of Grange-in-Borrowdale, hired a man and sent him down to the edge of Derwentwater early one morning to mow some grass. A neighbouring farmer said he'd heard a corncrake calling. "Nay," said Coates, "it's that farm man o' mine. He's doon at t'lake edge sharpening his scythe." The old men were particular. "You had to rake up to the hedges. Nothing was wasted."

In Borrowdale, when haytime was largely hand-work, the men even had to scale [strew] the hay by hand. Using forks for this job was not allowed. "I've been so stiff through bending down I was hardly able to walk downstairs next morning." Irishmen hired at Kendal or Hawes augmented the labour force. "Some of 'em walked to Mass at Kendal. They wouldn't miss going to Mass. If it wasn't good haytime weather, they got tight [drunk] and were locked up. They didn't want to be troubled by income tax so we paid them in notes."

The haytime men did not go short of food or drink. At Sawrey, Mrs Heelis [Beatrix Potter] bought a barrel of ale. In the Troutbeck valley, the men were provided with five or nine gallon barrels of beer which were purchased from a brewery at Kendal. "The best beer cost a shilling a gallon. Haytime beer could be bought for eightpence. It was taken to the meadow in stone bottles. Men drank it as they wished." Cheaper still was "botanic beer". Lakeland farmers' wives made lemonade.

Drinkings, the name for a ten o'clock snack consisting of a tea can and a lile basket with food, was served when mowing was over and grass that was lying must be "worked". At noon, a meal was served in the farmhouse. Tea would be "a bite and sup in the field, about 3-30... You had it while sitting behind a wall in t'shade." There was usually a good meal at the end of the day when the workers had washed and combed the hayseeds from their hair.

Just before haytime, someone was sent to the top field to collect the horse, which for the next month would be worked hard, harnessed to a sled or, later, to machines. The best type of horse for farm work stood at between 15 and 16 h.h. and was getting past its best at the age of twenty. You must humour a horse, which in summer literally worked from dawn till dusk. After a few hours' work, it was "loosed out" and given some feed. In sunny weather, the horse might be roused "gey soon". In Kentmere, "my father git back late from Brockstone clipping, which was followed by a party, then a dance. He had t'hosses in by 2-30 a.m. He yoked 'em up and as soon as it was light enough to see owt, away they went!"

Machines transformed haytime. An upper Lunesdale farmer bought one of the new-fangled side-delivery machines in April. By May, he could not restrain himself. He must see how it worked. He ordered his men to bring out hay from the barn. They strewed it across the corner of a field. The farmer harnessed the horse to the side-delivery and went happily, backwards and forwards, "rowing up" the hay.

In Great Langdale, when the last load had been transported to the barn, "you gave a halloa, like at a fox hunt. It echoed down the valley and told other families you'd finished haytime. Some of 'em would think: "They must a' rushed it.""

HOOK, LINE AND SINKER

Wilf Nicholson, of Ambleside, enjoyed rowing on Windermere with trawling rods and spinning minnow at about ten at night. He could enjoy this sport for about six weeks in the year and have some good trout to show for his efforts. He usually managed an average of three trout a night. The best fish he hooked and landed weighed five and a-half pounds.

When the six weeks had elapsed, Wilf met a visitor who was staying at *Waterhead Hotel*. He said he was returning to his home in Liverpool on the following day "and I'd love to take a trout back for the wife." Wilf humoured him, saying that he would like to go out but had no minnows. The visitor had some; they were cured golden sprats, each about six inches long. Wilf denounced them as no good. "In any case, they won't fit on the trout arch." The man looked so disappointed, an expedition with the sprats was arranged.

Wilf threw out the line as far from the boat as he could manage. He told the visitor to row and take in the slack. The line jerked. It must have caught on the bottom, thought Wilf. It was, indeed, a trout weighing three and three-quarter pounds. "There you are," said the visitor, "you don't know all about fishing." Wilf said it would not happen again. To prove his words, he tossed the line back into the water. Another fish was caught. When eventually they rowed to land, three fine trout lay on the bottom-boards.

The biggest tussle Wilf had was when he was in the company of Lanty Langhorn and pike were the prey. A whopper was struck off a beck-mouth. Lanty played it until his arms were tired. Wilf took over until he too was exhausted. They decided it should be beached. Lanty pulled out his jack-knife and stepped into waist-deep water. He lunged at the "fish" and shouted that he had got it. The knife was caught in a half-submerged larch bough. The hook had been caught fair and square in the middle. As the bough was dragged through the water it had given every indication there was a lusty fish.

Wilf's father had a sawmill at Winster. Whenever father and his workers were out of the district, Wilf and his friend Norman Hayton placed some wire netting at the bottom of the mill race and let out the water, filling a sack with trout which were sold (tuppence each) to the villagers. Father gave out a tremendous shout when, returning home, he found the mill dam was empty.

Every autumn, thousands of eels left Windermere, responding to a deep but mysterious migratory instinct that ultimately led them across the Atlantic to their breeding grounds in the Sargasso Sea. In the lake they had been "yellow" eels, dining voraciously on snails and insect larvae. A female was in fresh water for between ten and twelve years and before the migratory urge was upon them, they had changed colour to silver.

They travelled hopefully. By no means all of them arrived at their proper destination. At Newby Bridge was a simple but effective trap – a trap made of larch, renewed every ten or fifteen years. Each year, it accounted for no less than half a ton of eels which, transported alive in large metal containers, ended their lives in the bustle of a market at Manchester.

The trap was attached to the race that supplied water to the undershot wheel at a mill with a history that had been traced back to the fifteenth century. When it was not working, a sluice was opened. Water poured down an alternative course to the river, any eels being stopped by a grid, to be carried forward by a small amount of water into a wooden box about five feet long, two feet wide and two feet high. When I saw this trap, it was being operated by Mr H Leck. He had taken it over from John and William Knowles, natives of Staveley who moved to Newby Bridge as lads in 1881. They told me that their father, Roger Knowles, took over the *Swan Hotel* as well as the local mill; so it was not long before they were assisting at the eel trap. "Father would not eat an eel; it was the look of it that put him off. It was like a snake!"

Eels ran down the Leven to the sea chiefly in August and September. They favoured darkness and did not move even on moonlit nights. They liked wild, wet weather. On ideal nights for migration, two or three hundredweight of eels were collected. One night, in 1921, at about ten o'clock, after rain had been pouring for several hours, men went to inspect the trap and found it was so full of eels there was no room for the scoop used to transfer them to the "keep". The sluice gates were temporarily closed to stop more eels entering. Lanterns were produced and the men worked all night. The heaviest eel weighed seven pounds.

When elvers [young eels] were running up the Leven to Windermere in spring, they had no trouble in surmounting the weir for there was a "fish ladder" to help them. W R Calvert, a Cumberland writer, recalled the migration of elvers. He wrote: "Many of the boys and even some of the older men swore that these young eels developed from hairs from the tails, manes and fetlocks of horses watered in the beck or standing in it while the water-carts were being filled."

Autumn

The year might be declining but autumn was an especially busy time on the Lakeland farms. Young sheep were driven to more gentle country for the winter. Older sheep were salved in a laborious and hand-blackening process involving tar and grease. And a thwack heard on a calm autumn day might mean two rival tups had met, head to head, over a matter of which should serve the local ewes. In autumn, amid a flurry of tinted leaves and the first frosts, a new generation of sheep was assured.

On the high fells around Martindale and Thirlmere and in the deep woodland of Furness the red stags found their voices, proclaiming their presence to rivals and to the hinds they would serve.

Skeins of grey geese might be heard high above the dales of central Lakeland as birds from Iceland used an ancient flyway between the marshes of Solway and Lancashire.

There were gloriously clear and sunny days to show off the coppery hue of dying bracken fronds. Woodland trees donned their Joseph coats of many colours. Still water in lake and tarn held a mirror image of the landscape round about.

The tourist season ended and the folk of the Lake District settled back to their own round of social activity, such as Merry Neets. These were made up of spontaneous entertainment, with music provided by fiddle and accordion and tales to be told of fox-hunters of old, notably that old rogue John Peel, who wore a coat of undyed herdwick wool and roused the echoes on the broad acres of fell-country to the north of Skiddaw.

A SEASIDE INTERLUDE

In autumn, hoggs [lambs of the year] were driven from
the fell country to wintering areas in temperate areas,
often on the coastal marshes. To at least one farmer, it
was like a holiday – the only time he got away from his
home overnight." A Little Langdale farmer "walked 'em in
October, before tupping time. And, of course, we had to
walk 'em back. Hogg Day was fifth of April. Then you
settled up with farmers who'd kept sheep for you. I've paid
as little as five bob."

For sheep being wintered on the Solway flats, farmers and
their men stayed overnight at various farms en route. Some
six hundred hoggs were walked from Seathwaite to Solway
shore. Hoggs from Middle Fell, Langdale, were driven to
Whitbarrow, south of the fells. The first night of the journey
was spent in the Windermere area. The sheep were collected
about March 25.

THE SALVERS

Candles made of sheep-fat were used at salving time in
autumn. It took an hour to apply salve to the skin of
one sheep so work continued after dark. A candle was
clipped to the neb of a cap as a man worked in the confines
of an outbuilding. Salving a flock, a weary job spread over
several weeks, was in rapid decline about the start of the
Great War. It involved the "shedding" of wool and the appli-
cation to the skin of a mixture of Stockholm tar and grease,
with variants.

Any unsold butter was used in the salving house. In upper Lunesdale, a man remembered when some farmers had large pans and braziers for mixing the ingredients of salve, which "looked like liquid bacon fat and was brownly stuff." Salvers toured the farms; the best of them dealt with a dozen animals in a day. A "doctor" checked their work. He counted the sheds by parting the wool downwards. Herdwick Billy [Wilson] recalled that very little tar was necessary in making salve and that sometimes the grease used was poor quality butter.

At the start of the operation, the salver sat on a creel with the sheep beside him. Salve was poured into a long-handled wooden bowl which fitted into the side of the creel. The salver tipped the sheep on its side and parted the wool in strips, exposing the skin. At each phase of the operation, he dipped a finger into salve. When one "shed" had been dealt with, another was made beside it, and so on.

Salved sheep were said to winter better and to be averse to the attention of parasites. "They salved for pests but it didn't do much good... They'd just finished with it when I became a farm man about 1914." In Newlands, an old farmer salved "odd 'uns", using tar and a bit of mutton fat. Salving was replaced by sheep-dipping. "When they were to dip sheep at Seathwaite, two old men chopped wood for days on end and wheeled it to t'salving house. When you're dipping sheep, you should always dip at the same temperature as the day. They had a set-pot o' purpose at Seathwaite. Buckets of hot water from t'set-pot were poured into t'dipping tub."

Insect pests were still troublesome. At Troutbeck, when a sheep had become badly infested with maggots, "we clip't wool, poured Jeyes fluid on and that killed t'maggots. Then we rubbed sheep wi' whale oil to stop flies strikin' again."

COURTSHIP AND MARRIAGE

A suitor living at West Head, Thirlmere, walked "ower t'tops" to Grasmere, then "ower t'next fell", and met his girl at the top of Lingmell. "And he wouldn't have much time off – Sunday neet, likely." If lads from Shap started looking for girls at Bampton, the local lads hull'd 'em, a form of retaliation. It consisted of tying their hands behind their backs, blindfolding them and leaving them in the middle of a field.

Many a marriage sprang from a friendship established after church or chapel. "That's how boys and girls git mixed up i' those days. I can just see us now, at t'top o' t'hill, coming oot o' Kentmere church, all talking together, then setting off for home." At Troutbeck, "the only time I saw a girl was at week-end. Girls were hardly ever let out through t'week. T'lass I married lived at t'next farm, about three hundred yards from my spot. I went the same way home from church. As it happened, there were just the two of us going that way. That's how we got to know each other."

At Bampton: "I got my husband through being in the church choir. Our vicar used to say he'd got a courting choir – four lads, four lasses." Farm servants married during Whit-week, when they were due to have a week's holiday. It was one of the few times in their lives when they spent freely. After a wedding, the church gates would be tied and the bridegroom paid a toll, throwing money to the youngsters. At Chapel Stile, a rope was put across the road. It was considered lucky if someone with a piebald horse blocked the way with it.

A fortunate few went away on honeymoon, usually to Morecambe or Blackpool. Three members of one Whicham Valley family were married in the same year. "Only me and my husband went on a honeymoon." The most that an impoverished couple could expect was a short time spent with relatives not too far from home.

TOFFEE JOIN

Toffee was eaten at the festivities on November 5. Sometimes, two or three farming families would meet at one of the houses for a Toffee Join. The ingredients of the toffee were 1lb treacle; 1lb farm butter; 1lb brown sugar, a tablespoonful of vinegar and one of cold water. The toffee was boiled in an iron pan over the fire and a sample tested in cold water. When the toffee was cool enough to be handled, it was twisted – with buttered hands – into lengths about one and a half inches thick and four or five inches long. Some people liked it rolled in oatmeal. "It was just lovely to suck and crunch."

TUPPING TIME

One November, two insurance men had a fell farmer lined up for some policies he did not want. They met in a field where the farmer was giving the tups a bite of hay. The visitors arrived when he had half-foddered them. It was close to tupping time and - as he related to a neighbour – "the tips were getting restless. They looked gey fierce. I told yan of them insurance men: 'I hope you're insured, cos too's hungerin' them tips and I'se nut going to be responsible for 'em when they've eaten up.' They looked at t'sheep – an' took their hooks."

In autumn, tups began to break out and fight. "And, believe, me *do* they fight! I've known 'em neck one another. You'll see 'em go back a couple of hundred yards. Then they charge. You can hear t'crack o' skulls half way round t'parish... I wouldn't like to have my hand between their heads when they meet." Mug-tups [Suffolks or Wensleydales] were considered to be "fancy bred" and not able to stand much of a knock. At a farm near Coniston they told the story of a herdwick tup that put on "a bit of a spurt" when it saw a gate and crashed straight through. "It then walked on".

Old-time herdwick men prevented twinters [young sheep] from being mated by having small cloths – made from old clothes or coarse sacking - placed at their rear quarters. These cloths were known as "twinter-clouts". Taken off in spring, they were washed and ironed for use in another season.

Canon Rawnsley, a former vicar of Crosthwaite, Keswick, who was fascinated by fell farming, wrote that if any creature knew the miseries of headache it was surely a herdwick tup at mating time! There was something almost terrifying about a skull-to-skull collision between two determined tups, each weighing about a hundredweight. The wise farmer "held back t'tips an' shears", a reference to tupping and clipping. He kept the tups away from the ewes until a late date so that lambs would be born when the springtime weather was moderating. The shears were held back in early summer so the clipped sheep would not become chilled.

In autumn, a fell farmer visited a fair to hire tups and ensure the necessary "change of blood" in his flock. (Hired tups were returned to their owners in May). Esh'dl [Eskdale] Show took place on the last Saturday in September. Keswick Back End Fair was held on the first Saturday in October. A lesser-known Tup Fair, held at Orton on the second Friday in

October, was well patronised by local farmers. "Carts laden wi'tups set out from the fell districts the previous day. On Fair Day you could hardly get a horse into Orton..."

Some people transported tups by horse and trap but mostly the animals were walked. "T'owd tips nearly knew where they were going. They certainly knew what they were going for." You might get the use of a good tup for £1 in "olden time". Just before Eskdale Hirings, in t'owd days, farmers went on a round, from farm to farm, on what became known as Tup Sunday.

The best were "spokken for" in advance of a fair. Farmers keen to hire good stock visited such farms as West Head at Thirlmere, Glencoyne by Ullswater, Seathwaite and Gatesgarth. An interested farmer who visited Seathwaite usually contrived to turn up at dinner-time and was invited to tuck in to "summat roasted, maybe a couple o' legs o' mutton; also a great big rice pudding wi' raisins in it, followed by apple or currant pasty. And whisky."

Tups presented at the hiring fairs had their fleeces treated with red-rudd for the sake of appearance. John Hawell, a flockmaster who lived Skiddaw way, said that as the country's freedom depended on red-coated soldiers, so the freedom of the Lakeland fells was preserved by the red-fleeced herdwicks. "Red" brought down in bags from the appropriately-named Red Tarn was somewhat dull - a "bad-coloured red". Iron-ore was a major source of colouring until a special dye was available in powder form. Mixed with olive oil or water, depending on the weather, it was then smeared gently on the hairy coats of the tups.

Up to eighty tups might be walked to Esh'dl Show. Auld Isaac Thompson, of West Head, Thirlmere, took a week over the job. "He'd arrange for tups to be taken to Grasmere and they were then walked into Little Langdale. Next day they were taken over the passes to Esh'dul and on Friday they were assembled on the showground. Next day, they'd drive some fresh tups back to West Head." Tups being moved to the show from Seathwaite, at the head of Borrowdale, went by way of Sty Head and were quartered overnight at Wasdale Head.

A Little Langdale farmer who walked tups for seven miles from Fell Foot to Brotherilkeld arranged to deliver the animals at about 10 a.m. His father reckoned that the lad would be home again for milking at 5-30. "You never seemed to walk by yourself; there were plenty o' folk going to t'show."

When mating time arrived, ewes were gathered on the fell and transferred to handy fields near the farmhouse in batches of fifty or sixty, each batch having a tup allocated to it. Each tup was daubed on its underparts so that the course of the nuptials could be seen. One or two "jack tups" were loosed to make sure there would be a maximum lamb crop.

YONDER PHEASANT

The Lake District proper was not the best sort of country for game-birds. Yet for "nobs" like the Duke of Portland, a regular autumn visitor to the Underley Estate near Kirkby Lonsdale, no tract of land in Old England offered better sport among the pheasants than that around Lupton. He expressed this opinion to William Sims, who was head gamekeeper for forty years ago. William told me that at the dawn of the century, a man shot ninety-six pheasants in one stand.

Sensitive souls winced at the mass slaughter of reared birds but that was an age when, to quote from a popular harvest hymn, the rich man was at his castle and the poor man stood at his gate, the status of each having been decreed by the Lord. No one locally questioned the right of the landowner to do as he wished. Huge rural estates like Underley stabilised – some might say fossilised – local life, providing jobs and cottages for the many retainers.

Lord Henry Bentinck, who lived in the palatial Underley Hall, had grouse moors in upper Dentdale and dedicated the copses of Lupton to the pheasant, a gaudy bird that evolved in the forests of Asia. Lord Henry made the shooting as difficult as possible, encouraging them to fly high. He had sciatica and was conveyed to the woods in a four-wheeled carriage. According to Mr Sims, so moved was Lord Henry when a thousand pheasants had been shot before lunch that tears ran down his face.

The shooting party in 1902 consisted of Lord Henry, the Duke of Portland, Lord Elcho, Lord Charles Bentinck, Captain Lindsay, Mr Somers Somerset, Colonel Rhodes and the Hon G Gore. In the massacre of gamebirds – and any other wild thing that came into view - the barrels of the guns were almost too hot to handle. Of course, each had an attendant to do the loading. Also at their service were between eighty and ninety beaters, wearing white jackets, each beater being paid 3s.6d and provided with lunch. (The white jackets were washed in the evening ready for use on the following day).

November 13, 1902, was an unlucky day for no less than 1,579 pheasants. Also in the bag was a partridge, forty-four hares, four wild duck and forty-nine rabbits. In the previous two days, at Underley, 1,043 pheasants were slaughtered, with another 573 birds falling to the guns at The Warren. The total bag in three days was an awesome 4,142. Mr Woodhouse from Kirkby Lonsdale took away most of the pheasants for sale. A popular local chant was: "Up went £1 (the pheasant). Bang went a penny (the cartridge). And down came half-a-crown (the dead bird)."

FILLING THE LARDER

A Lakeland farmer might slaughter some old sheep, wethers, for winter eating. If left, they would have been just skin-and-bone by springtime. Sheep's head broth was a Lakeland delicacy. The skins of slaughtered sheep were cured with saltpetre and alum and made into mats or slung over the backs of chairs for extra comfort. The four to five pounds of fat in a slaughtered sheep were retained for weatherproofing boots or, rendered down, to be made into candles.

Visit a Lakeland farm kitchen at almost any time of the year and you would see sides and hams of pigs hanging from hooks driven into the oaken rafters. Almost every family kept a pig or two. A Kentmere man told me of a time when a sow was taken to the boar, which was at a farm over ten miles away. "We put the sow in a cart that had shelvings [detachable wooden frame] and a sheet over the top. Most of the piglets were sold off when they were fourteen weeks old."

At Keswick I was told that "some of those blooming great Cumberland pigs weighed about forty stone and had cheeks like lile hams." The biggest pig reared at Cunsey and "butchered" at Sawrey weighed 30 stone. Old-timers would not kill a pig until it had eaten a sixteen-stone bag of oatmeal. "You finished a pig off with oatmeal. That's where the flavour came from. We had oatmeal balls, or balls made of porridge, and fed them to the pig." In Mardale, the pig was fed on crowdie [lile potatoes], which were poured into a trough along with some blue [skimmed] milk.

A blocker [mallet] was used to stun the pig as it stood in the yard; it was then thrown on to a creel [bench of the type used at sheep-clipping time] where it was stuck [knifed]. "If it didn't drop first bat, us kiddies would be off to tell grand-dad that pig-killer had two shots at it." At Troutbeck, "I was dared to butch a pig. It was a little dark 'un, going off its legs. Chap I was with said: 'Bet thou daren't tackle it.' I said: 'There's nobody dare me.' I butchered the pig – and got the job ever after." The men helping with the pig-killing were handed mulled ale, which was beer with brown sugar and ginger, served piping hot.

William Middlesbrough, butcher at Newbiggin and a noted killer of pigs, travelled from farm to farm on ponyback and slew at least five pigs a day, charging half a crown a time. If a farmer wished him to return next day to cut up the carcass, an extra shilling was demanded. William was "as sharp as lightning". Two men who saw him perform at the *Plough Inn* at Lupton did not actually see the operation. The butcher distracted their attention for a few seconds by glanc-ing towards a field known as the Pleasure Ground and remarking: "Look at yon two chaps." The visitors looked up, saw no one, looked back – to find the pig was already dead.

At a farm near the head of Great Langdale, there was a dramatic interruption as the Martindale family's pig was about to be killed. Water was being boiled. Old William stood by with a bucket to catch and stir the blood. As the farmer and his neighbour, Jim Mitchell, were about to put the pig on the stool, the foxhounds came through the yard. The men let the pig go and went off with the hunt. The pig lived until Monday.

The pig's blood was drained into a bucket that had been previously warmed and also contained a handful of salt. Stirred continually so it would not coagulate, the blood was earmarked for black puddings, made by the farmer's wife, who would pour into the blood a quantity of milk, stirring it briskly. A pound of rice or groats, then some small pieces of fat, were added.

Seasoning consisted of thyme, marjoram, sage, pepper and more salt. All was laboriously mixed. "We had an old porridge stick, with two prongs. If the blood was beginning to go awkward, we forgot about the stick and put our hands in, with the fingers spread out. The basin of blood was set in front of the fire to keep warm till black puddings could be made." In grandmother's time, they were cooked in skins. Scraping the intestines was a messy, laborious job. "They were easy to turn yance you got a start, especially if you were working under a tap. Water would run through as easy as can be." The mixture, poured into small tins and placed in the oven, was cooked for two hours.

The dead pig was scraped, using warm water and a clean white cloth, and was then taken to the barn where it was hung up, shaved with a knife that had an edge to it like a razor and opened up. The pig was left hanging for a day before being cut up. Salting the major parts of the pig needed careful attention.

In Kentmere, "we did flitches flat, putting 'em on a table which we'd covered with a clean white cloth. There'd be a frying pan full of salt on the fire. That salt was hot and dry. Another bowl had cold salt and salt petre. You laid it on the table, got hot salt and spread it on meat about a quarter of an inch thick and rubbed till the pig side sweated. You then turned it over, got hot salt and sprinkled it all over, adding a gentle touch of sugar, then topping it off with cold salt.

"On top of that – sparingly - went the salt petre. You didn't want the meat to dry out too fast and it had to have the real taste. Then you did your hams and shoulders, working salt petre into the ends of the bones. You laid the meat on stone slabs. When it was ready it was washed down, then hung it up to dry."

Pig foot pie was a delicacy. "Our mother would scald and clean t'trotters – they boiled down like jelly – and she'd put some black pudding in t'pie. Being a pie, it had a crust on top." Jelly, bones and bits o' pig meat were too greasy for some Lakeland palates.

Bleak Midwinter

On the fells, snow squeaked underfoot. At night, when a silver moon hung like a lantern, there was little to hear but a tawny owl's hooting.

Winter was enlivened by straight drinking at the nearest pub, where you could get a pint of good ale for thruppence. One old chap poured ale on his breakfast porridge. Another, travelling from Langdale to Ambleside in a horse-drawn trap, had so much to drink he returned home kneeling in the trap, having such a bad attack of cramp he had to be assisted into his home.

A quarryman who regularly used a gated road on his way to the local inn ran into difficulties on a dark night. He put out his hand at what he considered to be the right place for the gate. The hand passed between two bars and he badly bruised his nose. Entering his favourite inn with a blooded nose, he remarked: "It's first time I knew my nose was longer than my arm."

Dances were lusty affairs, the premises varying in their size and suitability. At St John's school, between the Vale and Naddle, there was so little room for dancing that supper was served in the adjacent hearse-house, the space being temporarily cleared of the hearse. In Borrowdale, before the Institute was built, dances took place in the school or in the Mechanics' building near the Royal Oak. Joe Jenkinson played the fiddle and blind Joe Plaskett had a concertina. It cost a shilling to attend. If supper was provided, the charge was 1s.6d.

A MILLER'S LIFE

Davy Bank Mill, at Beckfoot, in the upper valley of the Lune, served farmers for miles around. Three lively streams united and in the headlong rush to the river an appreciable amount of water was diverted along a race leading to an overshot wheel that had a pitch-pine frame and buckets.

This was one of many little country mills. It had a good name for the grinding of oats and barley, some of it for domestic use and some to be used as feeding-stuffs for farm stock. The mill might be chilly in winter unless the worker, who clattered about in clogs, attended to the large coke fire at the kiln. Two sets of grindstones were in use – one set comprising French burrs, for maize and barley, the other a set of the softer Derbyshire Peaks, ideal for grinding oats. A prelude to the oatmeal season was dressing the stones by a bill, a sort of pick that operated in the grooves.

The Middleton family who owned the mill bought "potato oats", which had little husk. Ernest Middleton said: "You had to shell it but the main thing was to get it on to the drying kiln so it was really dry. You turned the stuff with a wooden shovel." Before Ernest was twelve years of age, he was sent out with horse and cart delivering feeding-stuffs – maize-meal for hens, ground linseed, whole linseed, barley meal for pigs, also bran, "sharps" and crushed oats for horses.

Maize was bought at the Liverpool docks, four tons at a time, and ground into maize-meal. Bran and "thirds" came from flour mills at Bootle. Before the Great War, the Middletons bought their oats at the Penrith corn market, which took place in the street, sacks of grain being set on ladder-like structures to raise them above the damp ground.

Transport to and from Penrith was by rail from Lowgill station, thence to the mill by horse and cart.

When threshing-time began in October, horse-drawn carts laden with grain arrived at the mill. A farmer identified his own sacks by putting his initials on them, adding the letters *rld* if he wanted his corn rolling. Among the best customers for oatmeal were local railway families. "When a signalmen finished a twelve-hour shifts, he'd get a bit of exercise walking down to the mill for a couple of stone of oatmeal. He'd sling the bag across his back and walk away."

At home his wife would make some oatcake on a backstone. The thinner you made it, the better. The backstone owned by the Middletons was fired using oat hulls [husks]. In later times, the hulls were bagged and taken to a firm in Liverpool who used them when packing crockery for export.

James Hayhurst, the jolly miller of Lupton, near Kirkby Lonsdale, was what they call a real country miller. "I takes water out o' t'beck and brings it down a race into t'mill dam so it's handy to my waterwheel. Farmers bring in oats and I dries and processes the stuff for 'em. I used to sell oatmeal in places as far apart as Barrow and Skipton." I was shown three pairs of stones – French burr, silver grey Kellett and Derbyshire. "We grind all that Old England grows – wheat, barley, corn, peas, beans, the lot."

In the early 1950s, James was running the mill with occasional help from his family. He also worked a small-holding. Lupton Mill originally processed wool that was transported to Bradford by pack-pony. "When they converted the mill to corn, they had to have a man to run it – didn't they? A practical man was wanted. So they gave t'job to one of my fore-elders who lived in Kirkby Lonsdale. He walked to the mill in the morning, looked after it, and walked home in the evening."

It was with joy that I followed James around the mill. I beheld the larger of two waterwheels, which had a diameter of twenty feet and was five feet wide, noting that the buckets were formed of pitch-pine. I saw an old backstone and an area where barley was laid to sprout before being used in malt. The oats were hauled aloft using a sixty feet long chain. The axle of the pulley was formed of the barrel of an old horse-pistol. In one of the rooms was an ancient muzzle-loading shotgun. The floor of the drying kiln held a sweet-smelling carpet of oats. A ton of oats. In calm conditions, the smell might have been detected half a mile away. Durham coal heated the kiln and the shovel that had worked on thousands of tons of grain was made of mahogany. "Lads used to laik [play] cards near the furnace at night. It's t'warmest shop in t'mill."

THE WHITE STUFF

Snow fell thickly and steadily – as "whisht an' as deftly as deeth [death]." At the merest hint of snow, the hill farmers were gathering sheep, which would be sluggish, disinclined to move far. Half an hour might be spent driving a small flock for a few hundred yards. Eddies of air swept the fell slopes and the flakes danced as though disinclined to settle. When the full force of a blizzard struck an area, the men plodded back to the farms, head down against the wind, as bemused as the sheep at the grim turn of the weather.

Some harrowing tales were told of men trapped by a snowfall and unable to reach home. Luckless farmers simply vanished from sight, their bodies being revealed weeks later as snow melted in gills and hollows. A man who reached home did so with frozen limbs and top clothes so stiff with the cold they were like suits of armour and must be beaten with a stick before they could be doffed.

On the fells, herdwicks sought shelter in the lee of walls or boulders. The snow swirled around them. When the storm abated, men went looking for overblown sheep.

If the snow remained crisp, they were safe for a while in their little snow caves, away from the biting wind and frost. A sheep's warm breath and the warmth of its body thawed a ventilation shaft By pawing at the ground, a trapped animal could exposed some herbage. If there was a sudden thaw, an animal might be smuddert [suffocated].

On the surface, tiny, brown-fringed holes in the snow indicated the position of overblown sheep. A sheep, sweating hard, gave off a strong odour that the dog could pick up. The daftest collies excelled at this work. A rod was used to probe the snow and a spade released the sheep. It was not wise to expose it suddenly to the freezing air after its snug snow quarters.

The collapse of a weak stretch of drystone wall indicated that a thaw was in progress. The eyes of the herdwicks brightened as they sniffed the air.

TWICE A DAY MILKING

In winter, a farmer – or his man - milked and foddered and mucked-out in a morning and evening. "You had always to be there." The cow-shed was handy to the house. Here was to be found a greeap [group], where the farmer put the muck from the cows. A carter visiting the saw-mill at Skelwith Bridge remarked to the owner: "I never knew that Tom Kirby grew grapes… he telled me he wanted some sawdust for his *greeaps.*"

The Shorthorn, a bonny cow, might be red or white or a mixture, which was roan. There was nothing prettier than a roan cow with its gentle colours. Around Buttermere, they wouldn't have white 'uns." A farmer bought or borrowed a bull and kept it for 'appen three years – "till he'd be covering his own offspring. That'd nivver do." A farmer liked a bull with horns "set right", extending outwards and turning in at the top. A Borrowdale farmer bought a bull at Cockermouth, "fetched it on t'train to Keswick and walked it from Keswick to Seathwaite." Other farmers took their stock to the bull. "They walked their stock for miles."

Some calves were kept as replacements. When a calf was born, the custard-like flush of milk – known as "beastings" – from the cow was collected by the housewife and made into an appetising pudding. In due course, a calf's diet consisted of skimmed milk and linseed. The servant girl usually fed the calves.

A good man was able to hand-milk twelve cows in an hour. The three-legged stool on which he sat was known as a coppy. "You could buy it at t'Co-op i' Gurt Langdale." A local man insisted on having a four-legged coppy. "Now and again, in summer, I milked a cow outside; I was too lazy to take it in. I went wi' t'cake and coppy and a bit o' cake in a tin."

A Rydal man who had a milk-round rose from his bed at about 5-30. His family, who helped with the milking, did not dally long for twice a day they were on the milk float that, twice a day, had an extensive milk round. "In the Great War, the charge for a pint was three ha'pence. It was measured straight from churn to the customers' jugs."

CHRISTMAS

Most Lakeland farmers kept geese – just a few, perhaps two or three geese and a gander. They were normally on sentry duty. "If anyone stirred of a neet-time, you'd hear t'geese shout." By December, the year's hatch had augmented the flock by thirty or forty young birds. They were severely culled for the Christmas trade.

A goose was speedily killed, then bled, the blood being used for black puddings. Plucking was an irksome job. "A goose has a top coat and a waistcoat, so it has to be plucked twice. Pulling feathers out is easy – but try pulling the blessed down." Goose feathers were dried off in a set-pot and then used for stuffing mattresses and pillows.

The birds kept by one Westmorland farmer were killed off and dressed on the same night. After the evening milking, the farmer, his family and men killed and plucked the geese. The blood was saved and groats added to make black puddings. On the following day, the bodies were scalded and trussed. Goose grease was grand for bronchial trouble. Fell lads greased their boots with it. The grease tended to go through t'uppers on to their socks.

A couple who fancied a goose rather than a turkey for Christmas eating ordered the bird from a neighbour. After several had been plucked, they were kept in the coldest room of the house. The farmer decided to take one of the dressed geese to be auctioned for Church funds. It had a transition from extreme coldness to the well-heated atmosphere of the church hall. The farmer, winning the goose, got it back. This was the bird the couple bought for Christmas. The bird was so warm it almost walked into the house. A strong smell of goose pervaded the rooms. "When cooked, it was the best goose we ever had."

Christmas Day saw the various meals run into each other. For the mid-day meal, there was goose and perhaps some Cumberland sweet pie, made from mutton "as fat as you could get", plus currants and raisins, sultanas, peel and brown sugar. "They put it in a dish, with a crust on it, and it was sweet – too rich for me. I couldn't do with it. You warmed it up every time you wanted it. The more often you warmed it up and the better it tasted. It got syrupy and went a dark colour."

In Little Langdale, "brandy butter's not much, but rum butter is grand; we often made some up for Christmas." Such butter was presented in "a little round bowl with a lid on."

LAST RITES

At the beginning of the century, an old woman would make sure a bag or case containing her funeral wear was handy. Such wear was often beautifully made, her white "nightdress" being embroidered. At Bampton, when Fanny Moffatt died, a basket was found under her bed. It contained a tape (to keep the mouth shut), scissors, socks, nightdress and handkerchief, also a piece of material to secure the feet. "There were two pennies for her eyes."

News of a death in the upper dales was made known when a relative personally bid people to the funeral. Bidding "began to fade out" in the Great War. It had been a foregone conclusion that every house was represented and on funeral day everyone wore black. But first there was the viewing of the corpse in a room of the house where the mirror was covered with a cloth. To see a corpse through a mirror was to invite bad luck.

In Little Langdale, "mother took us to the house on the night before they closed the coffin. I was told to place my hands on the brow of the dead person. If I did this, said mother, I wouldn't dream about it afterwards. Seeing a dead body didn't bother us kids. I had seen a few dead folk before I left school." When a baby died, "several of us went to the door and said: 'Please, we've come to see your baby.' The mother took us upstairs. There was this little thing lying in a coffin. She said: 'Put your hand on its forehead.' And this we did."

On funeral day, curtains at farms and cottages were drawn as a mark of respect. And after the graveside ceremony, mourners were invited to a special tea. In Great Langdale, "it was a damned good meal, with sandwiches, currant pasty and cake."

Towards the end of the nineteenth century, a young man who had worked in the stables of the Duke of Devonshire at Holker entered the business life of Lakeland. Operating from Grange-over-Sands with two carriages and two horses, Herbert Muncaster provided holiday trips into the district. With his brother Edward, he also made transport arrangements for hundreds of local funerals.

The funerals they attended were splendid affairs. The hearse, which had glass sides and was decorated with ostrich feathers, was quite modern for its day. A pair of black horses drew it to a cemetery that lay nearly two miles from the centre of what was then quite a small village. To hire the hearse cost the family of the deceased 35s. A carriage, no less immaculate, was available at between 25s and 30s.

The first carriage contained the clergyman. Then came the hearse, with the bearers walking by its side and the undertaker positioned immediately behind. When, at a large funeral, an unexpected halt was made, he walked into the back of the hearse and his shining silk hat was pushed down below the level of his ears. Later, the attendants had a carriage of their own. There might be up to four carriages bringing up the rear. For a posh funeral, a score of carriages would be mustered and each helper was provided with a pair of black gloves, a black tie and a black hat-band. Herbert Muncaster bought gloves by the boxful.

The man who drove the old-fashioned hearse at St John's in the Vale was particularly busy during the influenza epidemic that broke out after the Great War. "He took the hearse because he lived at the farm nearest the church. The hearse was a black box, embellished at the top, resting on four wheels."

Kids in Great Langdale were excited by the funeral of Grannie for they were allowed to "sit up wi' t'driver of the hearse." In Mardale, a bereaved family would provide the horse that drew the parochial hearse.

Lakeland Encounters

THE YELLOW EARL:
Opulence at Lowther

Before the Great War, a watcher on the heights of Shap might have seen Lord Lonsdale's special train chugging northwards with carriages – bright yellow carriages – reposing on some of the wagons. Whatever might be said of the Yellow Earl, he did things in style.

Hiring a special train to move servants, horses and carriages was part of the annual routine of Hugh Cecil, 5th Earl of Lonsdale, who wintered at Barleythorpe, in the hunting country of Leicestershire. He moved to London for the Season and then headed North to his vast estate at Lowther for grouse-shooting. His train used a special siding at Clifton and Lowther station where, in due course, and with great pomp, his senior staff greeted him.

Waiting to convey him to Lowther Castle was one of his celebrated yellow carriages, drawn by sprightly horses and complete with postilions wearing yellow uniforms and beaver hats. The first car at Lowther was a gift from the German Empress. He also offered Lordy a chauffeur, William Kieser, who remained in his service for years.

Lordy abhorred sloppiness. If anyone argued with him, they were in for a rough time. Yet despite his grand life and considerable fortune, he was a kindly man. John Peel, a long-time employee, who told me about him, said he was quietly spoken. It was "the gentlest voice you ever heard."

His nickname, Yellow Earl – which of course was never used to his face – was derived from the sandy hue of his hair rather than for his partially for yellow. This was a family colour long before he inherited the title. It was the Lonsdale yellow rather than the usual blue that denoted a Conservative in Westmorland.

John Peel, who worked for Lordy and rose to the position of head accountant on the Lowther estate, was a descendant of the famous huntsman and the son of a coachman in Lordy's employ. As accountant, he asked for (and received) a salary of £250 a year. Lord Lonsdale cautioned him to keep news of the appointment to himself until he had consulted the trustees, who must officially make the appointment. Said Lordy: "They usually do as I tell them."

The 365-room Lowther Castle presided over 4,000 acres of open country. Lordy had, by dint of absorbing a number of farms and removing the fences, transformed the landscape into the largest park in the land – larger, indeed, than exalted Windsor. The Kaiser, a guest in 1902, was fond of walking on the terrace that stretched before the grand façade of the castle. He covetously eyed the verdant parkland, wishing he could transport it to Germany.

Lordy bubbled over with pride in his immense tract of parkland. The estate maintained the roads that crossed it and trespassing off the roads was discouraged. Each morning a string of about twenty racehorses, most of which belonged to the Earl, were exercised on a course set out below the Terrace. To keep down the grass in summer, each local farmer sent ten to a dozen beasts, which were looked after by one or two estatemen. A ninety-acre tract known as The Meadow was fenced off and left ungrazed, the grass being converted into hay as winter fodder. Such was Lordy's pride in the big, open park that even if haytime had not been completed because of chancy weather, when he was due to return to Lowther the fences were removed. Lady Lonsdale's special pride was in a herd of about thirty Dexter cattle, which were milked in old stone-built byres.

John Peel, jnr., remembered Lowther in its heyday, when

it was a hive of activity, with scarcely a blade of grass out of place." Lordy lived at a good time for monied people, for taxes were low and there was a huge reserve of cheap labour. In his day, a country house, unlike the medieval castle, had facilities that made life tolerable. The head gamekeeper had to be at the Castle at 9 a.m. each weekday in case Lordy wanted to see him. He might stay all day without being summoned. The outdoor workers comprised thirty gardeners and fifteen gamekeepers.

Lord and Lady Lonsdale did much entertaining and a large kitchen staff travelled with them from house to house. Every two or three weeks, a beast and several sheep were slaughtered. If the Family was absent from Lowther, the meat was sent by rail to wherever they happened to be. In summer, even though the family was absent, Lowther was run by a resident butler and housekeeper, plus seven or eight housemaids. The castle had its own laundry, with half a dozen laundry maids.

It was in summer that coal and wood reserves were replenished. Special trains delivered to the local station coal hewn in his Lordship's pits at Whitehaven. From here it was transported to the castle to be stacked in the capacious cellars. Firewood was peeled oak, cut to fit the grates. Painters were kept busy and an upholsterer attended to the chairs and sofas.

In August, the grouse-shooters were conveyed in half a dozen carriages to moorland at Shap and Crosby Ravensworth. There was another tract in Bretherdale. Lunch was taken at some remote wooden shooting hut, where food – transported in a special wagon – was set out on white cloth. Footmen were in attendance.

The Yellow Earl rarely missed Grasmere Sports. Several days before the event, people and goods were despatched to Grasmere in a large stage-coach, followed by a farm wagon on which the canvas and props of his personal marquee were stacked. The great man travelled on Sports day in a wagonette.

He sometimes rode a dappled pony across country to Martindale, where he rented the deer-stalking from the Hasells of Dalemain. On a knoll overlooking the Nab was constructed a handsome wood-and-iron bungalow. Lowther Park had a stock of red and fallow deer. Donald Stewart and later his son John selectively culled the deer, taking the carcasses to be hung in a building at the hamlet of Whale. Venison from calves shot in the spring was especially tasty. Antlers from culled stags were taken to Sheffield to be fashioned into knife handles.

When, in later years, the Family spent Christmas at Lowther, the heads of department and important members of the staff were invited to the servants' ball held in the picture gallery. The under-dogs had their feast in the servants' hall. For the major event, food and drink were available in the steward's room. Lord and Lady Lonsdale stayed at the ball for an hour or two, chatting and having one or two dances. Then, as they were about to retire, he would say: "I hope you have a jolly evening. And God bless you all." Nearly every speech that Lordy made – even that at the local sheepdog trial – ended with the same invocation to the Almighty.

The Yellow Earl vacated Lowther Castle in 1936. The upkeep proved too much, even for him. He died at Barleythorpe in 1944. The fairy-tale castle except for its splendid façade was demolished. Memories of the Yellow Earl endured. When, years ago, I drove up Martindale in a yellow saloon car, the farmer remarked: "I had a shock when I first saw you. I thought Lordy was coming back…"

DELMAR BANNER:
Artist of the Mountain Tops

From the heights of Glaramara, I beheld a Lakeland on which man had made little impression and about which – on that day nearly half a century ago - few visitors would be aware. This was a roof-top Lakeland of misty fells, with a glimpse of green valley and grey lake. I saw an unbroken panorama, with the Langdale Pikes jutting up to meet the clouds on one side and, on the other, the high fells around Derwentwater.

My vantage point was not Glaramara but the centre of the "boys' room" at The Bield, in Little Langdale, the home of Delmar and Josephina Banner. The panorama, painted by Delmar from drawings made during a seven-hour stint on the summit of Glaramara, formed a frieze round three walls of the room. It demonstrated his fine sense of perspective. He had lightly wrapped the Lakeland fells in vapour. The desired matt finish had been obtained by mixing oil paint with petroleum.

Delmar Banner, though not physically strong, was a noted artist of the mountain tops. He spent hundreds of hours at high elevation, where mist sneaked round lichen-patterned boulders and the wind-sounds were complimented by the gruff voices of ravens. He took food but was inclined to forget it. Everything else was cleared from his mind as he composed a picture. He had a complete visual memory.

Drawing, an awareness of local geology and expressive design – these three formed the basis of his fell-painting. Delmar was entranced by the relationship between the solid, sculptural fells and the sea of air in which they swam. He joyously remarked: "It is the supreme character of the fells, as the eye tries to grasp them, that they are objects of solid rock, fire-tempered, ice-hewn and enduring through a long time. Yet, also, they are distant, mysterious, swimming in a sea of light and air and light and colour that shifts and dissolves and obscures."

Delmar could paint air. Damp Lakeland air held the light in a curious way. "The identical never recurs," said the artist. "Even typically similar conditions may not recur during a whole season or for years. Many of the events of mountain nature most worthy of record are past in a few moments." He preferred to look down or across at a mountainous landscape rather than from a seat in the dale. (Heaton Cooper, another fine Lakeland artist, told me much the same thing. And he, like Delmar, was not upset by adverse weather. No day was good or bad – it was simply dry or wet).

On his return home, Delmar was invariably very tired. The drawings and colour notes he had made out-of-doors, using oil or chalk, were beside him as he did the actual painting in his studio, a former bracken loft.

Delmar and Josephina, his Argentine-born wife, met during student days at the Regent Street Polytechnic in London. The frieze I admired in the old farmstead on the fellside in Little Langdale was painted when, living in Sussex, they were homesick for the mountains. Determined to live in the Lake District, they acquired The Bield, a three centuries' old farmstead that was being vacated by Fleming Mawson. He was keen that under a new owner the character of the building, with its oaken beams and cupboards, its mullion windows and flagged floors, would be maintained.

Bield means shelter. Ancient yews and oaks moderated the fury of the northerly wind. The farmstead, built of mortarless stones that were stoped so as to reject the rain, was snug in winter and cool in summer. The thick walls were the nesting places of mice and wild birds. Water came from a spring, intercepted by a tank set on the hillside – in effect, it was being supplied by Lord Muncaster – and in the absence of electricity, the Banners used candles and tilly-lamps, which worked on paraffin. Oven and boiler, in cast-iron, flanked the fireplace.

The huge painting of the view from Glaramara that adorned one of the rooms, and had begun with sketches and notes made in situ, accompanied them to Lakeland in 1940. Now Delmar had the gracious manner of one who had found peace with the world. Art and nature were not enough. Delmar was an Anglican lay reader. Several of his paintings had found a home in churches and colleges. He had a collection of paintings made in Palestine. Delmar's portrait of Mrs Heelis (Beatrix Potter) showed her clad in homespun clothes and with a backdrop of a Lakeland showfield.

When Delmar died, Josephina moved several times. I visited her when she had a cottage in the upper part of Ambleside. A fellow guest for afternoon tea was Heaton Cooper. Another time, with Nigel Holmes of *Radio Cumbria*, I was invited into a studio-cum-living quarters, tucked out of sight of the world behind a high wall, not far from the cottage where she had recently lived.

At the age of ninety-one, Josephina was still sculpting. Big blocks of stone were lifted over the wall by mobile crane. In the previous summer, having been invited to open an exhibition at Rydal Hall, a centre for Carlisle Diocese, she had arrived early to see sculpting possibilities in the stump of a dead tree. She offered to buy the stump and was, of course, given it without charge. It would have to be split lengthways, in three equal parts, in order to get it through her studio door.

She worked with wood indoors and stone out-of-doors, wrapping rags round the handles of the chisels to make them round and soft. "They are then quite easy to hold. I can work all day." How did she find the strength to do major work? "I am quite young inside and old outside. I find that being old is rather like feeling as you do after an operation in hospital. You wonder why you're so weak...It isn't so much a matter of strength; it is one of rhythm. I've done this work for many years...It's not a strain; it's just a pleasant exercise."

The building, thick-walled and strong, was rooted on rock. William Green, an early Lakeland artist, had drawn it when it stood beside a grassy track used by travellers from Ambleside to Kirkstone Pass. She believed it was the home of a shepherd. In the room where she lived, worked and had her being, I was astonished to find that a third of the space was occupied by a grand piano, "my pearl of great price – my black pearl – being French and one hundred years old. I've loved it."

As her guest for a few hours I had a cup of tea, a piece of cake and a conversation in which she did not waste a single word. Then, once more, I stepped through the door in the high wall, re-entering (with misgivings) a strident modern world.

Loweswater

WILLIAM WILSON:
Champion of the Herdwick

The roadman rested an elbow on the handle of his spade. "William Wilson?" he queried. There was a pause, as though he was letting the words roll around his mind. I added: "They also call him Herdwick Billy." A smile creased the roadman's face. "Why didn't thou say so?" he remonstrated.

With a few hurried phrases he directed me to *Herdwick View*, a detached house standing in the fertile Derwent Valley, not far from the outflow of Bassenthwaite Lake.

William Wilson, sheep farmer, took up residence here in the early 1930s, his obsession with herdwicks leading him to commission stained glass studies of the breed. He soon had a stock of these distinctive Lakeland sheep on Binsey Fell.

I first met him in 1958. A stocky man, he wore tweedy clothes, a floppy trilby, well-used mac and well-polished boots. A moustache of coarse grey hair adorned his face. He had a cheerful expression. Herdwick Billy was born at Wood How Farm, Nether Wasdale, in the far west of the Lake District. The farm, with its stock of four hundred herdwicks, was let to his father who ran an extra one or two hundred sheep. Those additional sheep were his property – and profit. When he left the farm, he must ensure that four hundred herdwicks remained to maintain the vital heaf-going instinct.

The Wilsons moved to the head of Wasdale, where father ran three farms. His son was so keen on the herdwick breed of sheep he was inclined to play truant from school in order to spend more time with them. He was nobbut a lad when father gave him a lamb to rear. Inevitably it was known as

"Billy's ewe". She mothered some fine tups. William was secretary of the Herdwick Sheep Breeders' Association when the first Flock Book was brought out in 1920. He remarked: "There was some work in it, I can tell you."

For twenty years, this cheerful champion of Lakeland sheep farmed at Watendlath, the lile hamlet tucked out of sight of the world, approached by road from near Keswick. He had a stock of 3,000 sheep. About 1927, keen to wed a hill farm to a lowland farm, he took over Stoneycroft in Newlands, where he lived, and Ashness Farm, which was managed by one of his nephews. With this arrangement, his ewes thrived and the hoggs [young sheep] had a good start before being turned on to the scanty pasture of the fell.

He gave up both Ashness and Stoneycroft and bought *Herdwick View*. It was in the lounge, with the stained-glass herdwicks winking down at me, that he yarned about the breed. It throve on "the sweet herbs of the fells" in areas where many another breed of sheep would hunger. The only time he was "pushed to fodder 'em" was in the tremendous bad winter of 1917, when he was at Watendlath. "a real high-lying place." A herdwick is hardy, said Herdwick Billy. "I've known a sheep be covered by snow for twenty-one days and recover. I'd put the Scotch black-face next to the herdwick for toughness."

His knowledge of the breed was such he was called to evaluate sheep with a change of tenant at one of the farms in the high dale country. At a Lakeland show, he had soon picked out the best of the breed. "Many of the old-time sheep judges went by the eye; it must be bright and sharp. The ears must be sharp. A sheep's no good if an ear hangs down like that of a hound. The ribs should be well-sprung." An extra rib was claimed for a flock at the top end of the Duddon Valley.

STANLEY WATSON:
Mountaineer

Rock-climbing became popular in Lakeland about the 1860s, though Atkinson, an Ennerdale cooper, had challenged the crags when climbing Pillar Rock by the old west route as early as 1826. A pioneer of the sport was W P Haskett-Smith. In the early 1900s, a Frenchman established himself as a rock-climbing guide at Wasdale Head.

Early climbers, wearing Norfolk jackets, breeches and long stockings, used nailed boots and hempen rope until, in the 1920s, boots began to give way to plimsols, which were more sensitive. When I met Stanley Watson in 1956, the tendency was for long ski-trousers and windjammers, for nylon ropes and shoes of hard composition rubber, as worn by Commandoes during the war.

Stanley, a gentle, modest man, fell in love with the crags of Lakeland as a visitor from his home at Tynemouth. He had the usual, almost common, experience of being trapped in Piers Ghyll with darkness approaching. After spending a night up there, he managed to get out without assistance. His brother had the same adventure twenty years before.

Stanley did much for mountaineering in 1930 when he founded the British Mountain Guides and had a climbing school at Newton Place in Borrowdale. During the ten years of its existence, none of his clients suffered injury on the rocks – though some had mishaps while using gymnastic appliances set up in the garden. An outspoken pupil who had been questioning one of Stanley's assistants, asked: "What happens if the rope breaks?" Said the assistant: "Don't worry about it. We've plenty of ropes at home."

Great Gable was his favourite mountain. The climbs, facing south, were clean. A climber had the benefit of the sunlight and was free from moss and water. Stanley climbed Kern Knotts when blindfolded. Once, on Helvellyn with three friends, a sudden blizzard reduced visibility to a foot or two. Lasting snow meant they could not keep their eyes open for long. The climbers roped themselves together and felt their way off the mountain with their eyes shut. Said Stanley: "I could not believe there could be such conditions on a little 3,000 ft peak." Once, when he was pioneering a new hazardous climb with assistants, he stood on a companion's head to get a two-finger hold that enabled him to continue.

Rock-climbing has its lighter moments. Stanley, whose happy expression was "the greater the firma, the less the terra", told me of two entries about Pillar Rock from a record book kept at Wasdale Head. The first simply stated: "To-day I ascended the pillar in three hours and found the rocks very soft." A wag had written underneath this item: "To-day I descended Pillar in three seconds and found the rocks very hard."

I asked him why people should take the most difficult route up a mountain. He regarded the sport as a form of madness – a tempting of Providence not in accordance with "safety first." Yet to the cragsman, finally perched above the world like an eagle, triumphant from a struggle with his bare hands, came a wild joy of mastery; of independence and aloofness.

It was a sense of self-sufficiency, elemental and perhaps barbaric, "but extraordinarily thrilling and indescribably satisfying."

JOHN BOWNASS:
Quarryman

About five o' clock one grey evening, many years ago, two horse-drawn carts laden with furniture rumbled into Little Langdale. The Bownass family – parents and eight children – was returning to their native dale after a spell in Borrowdale during which father had been black-smith at Honister slate quarries. The carts were dusty. The weary horses had begun the journey at Keswick thirteen hours before.

John Bownass, one of the younger-end of the family, walked to his new home over Stake Pass in the company of a man who lodged with them. John was twelve years of age when he started work at the green slate quarry on Honister. He was employed as an office boy for a shilling a day. Then he was set to work riving [splitting] pieces of slate to a size and thickness appropriate for roofing. An accident in the quarry kept him in hospital for a year. He resumed work at a time when no work meant no pay.

Having served his apprenticeship, John was paid five shillings for a full working day. The average wage at that time was 4s.6d. The quarries lay over two miles from his home in the dale; he began work at 7 a.m. and "knocked off" at 5-30 p.m., at which time he began the long walk home. The quarrymen had a few days off at Easter and Christmas but, not being paid for time off, they were glad to be back at work.

At Honister, the slate they quarried and trimmed for use was transported to Keswick by horse and cart. The company owned seventeen such outfits. Carts were kept under control on the steep hill into Borrowdale by the tightening of a screw on the axle tree. A carter would manage only a single journey a day. A good "river" produced four slates from every inch of good rock. John found the rock "bad to handle in winter when the frost was on. It used to nip your finger ends and make them sore."

In Little Langdale, the quarrymen were a sturdy, independent breed. Their large families seemed to thrive even though the amount being earned for each household was paltry. When the Bowness family returned to the dale, John – with six years experience – had no difficulty in getting a job at the quarries.

Most of the two hundred or so men arranged bargains with the quarry-owners and were paid at so much a ton, a deduction being made for the cost of powder and other necessities. Allowance was made for quality work and, conversely, less was paid for poor stuff. The grades were classified as best, seconds, best peg and second peg. The roughest slate was called "Tom". In a fine spell, John and two men earned about 6s.4d. a day "but when the month-end came the boss knocked our price down. If you could make 5s a day, you were all right. It was slightly more than the pay of day men.

As at Honister, horse-drawn carts were used to transport the slate. From Little Langdale, most of it was taken to the railway stations at Windermere and Coniston. A cart could manage two journeys in the day if the destination was Coniston. Slate trimmed for roofing purposes was bringing the quarry owners between £7 and £10 a ton. Trade slackened when cheaper roofing materials were being marketed.

Quarrymen worked hard and also played hard. Quoits were popular on a summer evening. In winter, a melodian or fiddle was played at dances. A diversion was provided by fox-hunting. Both Anthony Chapman and William Porter brought hounds to the district – and then the quarrymen were inclined to slip from their work for a day's sport. When the boss saw men sloping off, he shouted: "Has them yowling things com'd again?"

When hounds were kennelled at a local inn, John Bownass left his home at Stang End to join them for a day's sport. William Porter wanted him to join him for supper but John insisted he must return home or his wife would be worried about him. As he entered his home, she exclaimed: "Here thou comes again – as drunk as a hullet [owl]." In fact, he had nothing to eat or drink since morning. "It was the longest day I ever had. My windswept hair was standing on end. I must have looked wild..."

JOSEPH HARDMAN:
Photographer

The physical beauties of Lakeland cannot be catalogued like lots in a sale. Binding and merging them into a picture that refreshes the mind and stirs the soul are the vagaries of light, such as the sunlight that inflames acres of dead bracken fronds on the wintry hills and makes the waters sparkle. Joseph Hardman was happy to be out and about in Lakeland on most days of the week, fixing the ever-changing moods of the landscape on photographic plates.

A heavily-built, fresh-faced man, he accumulated over 50,000 negatives and stacks of glossy magazines and newspapers in which his work appeared. When I was editing the magazine *Cumbria*, the receipt of a batch of whole-plate, glossy prints from J Hardman, Kendal, was an almost weekly occurrence. Hardman prints graced the first issue of the new series in 1951 and appeared regularly down the years. His photographs were never flat, taken with the sun tanning the back of his neck. Crags or trees, animals or people, were used to create striking patterns.

Glance at one of his monochrome prints and you might tell the time of the day and the season of the year in which it had been taken. He was a master of taking pictures against the light. He was not discouraged, like many photographers, when the shadows lengthened and the light began to fade. There was always, for Joseph Hardman, that odd shaft of sunlight to bring up the subject against a dark background. Thousands of negatives were concerned with Lakeland farming, taken before the time of radical change. He lost a camera, which might still lie at the bottom of the plunge pool at Skelwith Falls.

I corresponded with Joseph Hardman frequently and used hundred of his pictures but only once did I see him at work. His wife set up the heavy tripod just across the road from the church at Bowness. Carefully, he attached to it a large plate camera. This would be no "snapshot" but a carefully posed study. He waited until the lighting conditions were right. The photograph was exposed, the plate sheathed, removed and replaced with another. It was a languid, thoughtful operation.

Joseph Hardman was born at Radcliffe, near Manchester, in 1897. He became a "half-timer" at a factory producing shuttles for the cotton mills. His weekly wage was 1s.10d (if he worked afternoons) or 3s.4d (for the mornings). At fourteen he was on a man's wage, which was not much. Like many another ambitious Lancashire lad, he emigrated – to Westmorland – and became a member of the Kendal Photographic Society. Soon he had given up his daily work to devote himself full-time to photography.

This was not the normal commercial photography, involving babies, school and wedding groups. Joseph Hardman went for pictures that might make good book illustrations or be suitable for reproduction in newspapers and magazines. He was fond of remarking: "When you're taking portraits, the model can talk back. When you're taking a landscape, you can please yourself."

He travelled about the Lake District in a car driven by a friend or he hired a taxi. Sometimes he covered two hundred miles a day. "I think I can do better when I'm in the back of a car... I don't miss much then." Evenings were spent in the darkroom. He had no assistant as he developed and printed up to five dozen photographic plates.

Walking did not appeal to a man who once weighed nineteen stones and managed to slim until he made the scales dip at sixteen. He liked the fells best, not as a walker, but framed by a car window. He and his assistant (his wife) were seen at social events like shepherds' meets and agricultural shows. He photographed the Mardale shepherds' meet when it was held at the *Dun Bull*. That was before the valley was inundated as a reservoir to serve the needs of thirsty Manchester. He had some fine studies of bearded Isaac Cookson, of Helton, who had attended Mardale meets for sixty-one years.

Joseph Hardman's intense knowledge of Lakeland in all seasons led him to be first with photographs of snowdrops and wild daffodils. If he wanted a picture of Langdale, he knew he must be there early in the morning because little sunlight reached the dale after two o'clock until the the days lengthened towards the end of January. He took photographs of an impressive migration of sheep that wintered on the Cartmel Fells and in April were driven home to Hawes in Wensleydale, a distance of over forty miles, the journey taking two days. The huge flock, keeping to a strict timetable, passed Kendal Town Hall at twelve noon, reaching Sedbergh, the first halt, about five.

He and his wife relaxed occasionally at Berners Close, Grange-over-Sands. Their holidays were spent at – Blackpool.

JIM WETTON:

Days on the Peat Moss

Jim and I sat beside his peat fire at Whitbarrow Cottage, his home since 1946. Blue-grey smoke curled lazily from the turves that soon would have a cherry-red glow, persuading us to move back our chairs. A visit to Jim Wetton would have been memorable if only for the reek of peat. I also had keen anticipation about what he might tell me of Whitbarrow Scar and the adjacent Foulshaw, an area of mossland just north of Morecambe Bay.

Jim, returning to his native district after war service, married, found a job on Whitbarrow Lodge estate, a home at Parkside, which stands just above the imposing Lodge – and kept his fuel bills low by exercising a right to cut peat on the mosses. He retired from work in 1983 after fifty-one years' service. When I first met Jim, he was solitary but never lonely, having many good friends and a profound interest in the natural world about him.

His father, Harry Wetton, had moved from Pilling to Whitbarrow in 1923. As a young man, Jim was expected to give a hand with the peats. A special barrow was used. "My brother used the barrow to take them to the stack and I threw them up to father." A peat stack was ten feet by six feet "and maybe seven feet high." The peats were laid flat and at intervals layers of dead bracken or sticks were put in to stabilise the stack. The estate horseman carted the dry peat from moss to Parkside, where the peat-house had a capacity of about 5,000 turves. "He used an ordinary cart with high sides attached. The peats were light. We could get maybe 800 at a time into the cart."

When I first visited Jim in his Whitbarrow cottage, he did

not make a fire in summer and used peat and logs the long winter through. All that was needed, first thing in the morning, was to stir up the red ashes, apply the air from a pair of bellows and add some more peat. Such a fire was truly hot. Joe Fletcher, an old-time blacksmith at Gilpin Bridge, fired with peat when fitting metal hoops to cart wheels.

One Maytime I watched Jim (and others) cutting peat on Foulshaw Moss. He was slicing turves from a deep face. At first, in their dark wetness, they resembled chocolate cake. Jim was soon spreading them out to let the wind and the sunshine – mainly the wind – reduce the moisture content. He would then make a *windrow*, a structure six or seven peats deep, arranging the peats so that "the wind can get between them."

Hopefully, by the end of October, his little wood-and-zinc shed by the mosses would be full of stacked peat – up to 7,000 peats for household use. He did not want them to stay out in cold, wet weather and told me that when frozen a peat goes twice as thick as it should be. Jim said that before the huts were built, dry peats were put in large sacks. The best way to stack peat in a shed was to build a wall at the front – and throw them in. "Don't stack 'em in or the air can't get among them. Peat is like hay. Once you put it into a shed, it'll start and sweat and then dry out – just like hay in a barn."

A peat must be damp when put in storage or it would break up. The drying process continued under cover. He transferred peats from shed to the peat-house beside his cottage in batches of 1,000. In a dry, breezy season the peat might be usable in five weeks. Peats must be damp when put in storage. Otherwise they would begin to break up. Domestically, he used a lot of wood. Ash was the best. "Peats by themselves throw out heat but don't last as long as wood and peat together."

Some people, seeing Jim at work on the mosses, asked if

he could supply them with peat for their garden. Jim said that this type of peat would not be any good until it had been burnt to dust. He called the top layer of peat *fey*. Underneath lay grey peat, which he described as "fuzzy". Lower down was black peat – the best type of fuel. And lower still was *short metal*, with a brown hue. "It doesn't hold together." Then came more "greyish stuff" and finally the clay.

Jim was well-acquainted with local folk lore. He had heard of a road that crossed the Moss and was made using bundles of faggots. It was good enough to take horses and carriages. When conditions were right, it was a good approach to the Kent estuary at a point where it might be forded to Sandside.

School lads smoked peat. The bowl of their pipe was made of elderberry from which the pith had been removed. The stem was fashioned from a piece of honeysuckle. When Jim was turning peats, he usually saw lizards "scampering about...the little beggers can bite if you're not careful." Twice he had found a lizard in peat he was about to put on the fire. Jim would coax a lizard on to his shovel and take it outdoors.

He recalled with pleasure his young days when everywhere there was the reek of peat. Every farm had a peat fire – and a pair of bellows to resuscitate it in the morning.

SIDNEY COLE
Farmer and Folklorist

Thirty years ago, Sidney was a regular contributor to *Cumbria*. He had a series of notes and pictures relating to country bygones; they were published under the title of "T'Owd Days". Visiting him at Knocker, his home at Caldbeck, "back o' Skiddaw", I was shown his fine collection of rural bygones and heard him describe farming conditions when hand operations were the rule and there was a large reservoir of cheap labour.

But first – this being Sidney – he explained the unusual name of his house. Formerly there were two cottages. In a semi-industrialised village, one of them held the knocker-up. I should remember that lead-miners working up Roughton Gill set off to walk there at between 5 a.m. and 7 a.m. The rap of the knocker-up's cane against a bedroom window had roused them from their sleep.

When Sidney arrived at Caldbeck in 1913, there was one binding machine, which belonged to Chris Hewetson. Otherwise, families harvested with the ordinary reaper and the sheaves were hand-tied. Sidney had ploughed with a swing plough and he remembered when old Andrew Scott mowed a three and a-half acre field with a scythe. Caldbeck, in common with many another large rural village, had a lot of poor housing. People clattered about in clogs. A man bought a new suit every five or even ten years.

A Northumbrian, he eventually became established at Brownrigg, a farm with buildings set on the 1,000 ft contour. It was none the less a good farm. The land was loam on limestone. Dora, his wife, recalled that in 1919 the only source of water was a well at the back of the house "and the heavens above." An oil lamp with a single burner provided the illumination.

Such a farm carried a small quantity of stock. "You were thought to be in a big way if you had twenty-five cows and six or eight cows. Income tax was gauged at double the rent and anything a man might make over that sum – he kept. Rates were 1s.11d in the pound. Transport was cheap. A farmer might have a 'spring cart' – a cross between a buggy and a heavy cart – and we walked all our stock to Wigton. You'd take the horse and cart there once a fortnight for essential purchases. A pair of horses I bought lasted me thirty years before they were finished; they had scarcely cost me a halfpenny…"

The mid-day meal was often tatie pot – "potatoes with a bit o' meat dragged through it." It could be tasty, however. Men working in the field had tea out-of-doors at about 3 p.m. When the day's work was done, the horses were watered and fed, and the cows milked, and the horses bedded down, before the workers received their evening meal.

When scythes and simple machines were used at haytime, there was an elaborate system of making foot-cock, cock and pike to protect the hay in chancy weather. Farmers never "cut ahead of themselves". A man who "slapped every field down" courted disaster for he had no rapid means of getting the hay under cover. Lads from Cumberland, where haytime was later than in Westmorland, offered their skills and energy to Westmorland farmers for a month, receiving between £15 and £20, with board and lodging provided.

Sidney took his first photographs when he was young and built up a collection of cameras showing the development of what was to be called "the only new folk art of the twenti-eth century." He began to collect the unwanted objects from farms and cottages in about 1947. If he came across an object worth preserving, often among a farmer's lumber, he offered to buy it. In due course, he began to talk about his collection to local organisations. He was amused when the chairwoman of a Women's Institute introduced him as "Mr Cole and his Bits and Pieces."

TIMOTHY TYSON:
A Walking Boot-maker

When her father died, a Langdale woman walked over Wrynose and Hardknott passes to Boot, in Eskdale, to attend the funeral. She carried her infant son. After the funeral, she was driven by horse and trap to the top of Hardknott and from there walked home, carrying the child. Timothy Tyson, the Grasmere boot-maker, told me this story when I met him in 1957. He could vouch for its accuracy. The woman concerned was his aunt. When Timothy was four years old, his mother took him from Irton, where he was born, over Muncaster Fell end to Waberthwaite, to be measured for some shoes by Moses Dodgson. New snow had covered the tracks. For a time they were lost.

Said the cheerful Grasmere boot-maker: "In my young days, walking was about the only way of getting about. Farmers had their horses and traps, some folk had bicycles but ordinary folk relied on Shanks Pony." Tom Jackson, of Ambleside, would set off from his home with his youngers on on a Sunday morning to visit friends in Borrowdale. The youngest child had to be carried.

In contrast was Timothy Tyson's story of a man from Nether Wasdale who courted a lass at Wasdale Head. The parents of the girl did not take kindly to him, so on courting-neet he waited until they had gone to bed, took of his boots at the door and crept quietly into the house. A local lad, knowing of this, smeared his boots with aniseed. After the suitor had got part way home, the hounds were released. The walker, hearing their music, put on a spurt and got into his house just before they reached him.

The Tyson family were great walkers. "I've never put up any records but I've done some decent walks." He had been to the summit of every notable Lakeland peak and after he had celebrated his fiftieth birthday he climbed in many parts of Scotland, bagging over three hundred Munro's [peaks over 3,000 ft]. His work as a boot-maker meant that his walking was restricted to Sundays, in winter, at one time covering between thirty and fifty miles in the day. One of his nice day's walks from Grasmere took in Borrowdale, Gatesgarth at the head of Buttermere, Scarth Gap, Black Sail, Burnmoor, Birker Moor, up Ulpha and over Walna Scar to Coniston, from where he returned to his Grasmere home.

Black Combe was a favourite hill because of the impressive views round about, including – in sharp conditions – eminences in England, Scotland, Ireland and Wales. Timothy had witnessed the Spectre of the Brocken three times. Sunlight cast his shadow on a bank of mist in gigantic proportions and surrounded by a halo of rainbow hues.

He remembered seeing the first car being driven up Eskdale on the day of the Tup Show at the *Woolpack* in 1899. About that time, penny-farthing bikes were still in evidence though many people were now buying "grids", which had cushioned tyres. Some visitors to Irton Hall, then the home of Sir Thomas Brocklebank, brought with them a bicycle made for four. They raced it up and down the avenue. When they took this fabulous machine on to ordinary roads in Lakeland, it was so long it scraped the hump-backed bridges.

Seeing Timothy Tyson at work in his little shop, you would not suspect that his interests, apart from boot-making and repairing lay on the hills of Britain. He was also a great swimmer in Lakeland tarns.

Castleberg
Book List

If you have enjoyed reading this book, you will be interested in our other publications. On the logo (above), the horn of a herdwick sheep, traditional breed of the Lake District, forms the "C" of Castleberg and reflects the north-country nature of books we publish. The author of each book is W R Mitchell.

BIOGRAPHY

The portrait is of Richard Kearton, who with his brother Cherry, pioneered wildlife photography. Read about the exciting careers of these natives of Swaledale in WATCH THE BIRDIE, a recent Castleberg publication. Lakeland is represented by Mrs Heelis (much better-known as Beatrix Potter). Our book, based on taped interviews with those who knew her, gives an account of the real woman and is in contrast with the many glamorous accounts of her life. See our list of mini-biographies for facets of the lives of a quartet of fascinating people.

RAILWAYS

Castleberg has published books about the Settle-Carlisle railway for forty years. The current offerings include two with a generous picture content, one dealing with Ribblehead viaduct and the other detailing the construction period in the 1870s. Notice also our book on Garsdale, an account of a railway community, and a light-hearted collection of a hundred tales of the famous line.

A New Book

HOW THEY LIVED IN THE YORKSHIRE DALES

In the dale-country of a century and more ago, money was scarce. As t'owd chap said: "I've done owt but mak a fortune and I was never much good at that." This well-illustrated book deals with aspects of Dales life through the year. The style is anecdotal and there is much humour.

Hubberholme Church

HERITAGE

Our drawing, of the coal man, is from LIFE IN THE LANCASHIRE MILLTOWNS. Many of our books have had a folksy content – we tend to put people before things – and we specially recommend the very readable MUSIC OF THE YORKSHIRE DALES, which includes potted biographies of a trio of musical greats – Elgar, Delius, Quilter – each of whom got to know the dale-country.

NATURE

Our popular works on birds of the Yorkshire Dales and Lake District are for those who lack a specialist knowledge of the subject but would like to know more about the birds they see on country jaunts. The books have been illustrated by David Binns, one of the best bird artists, as you will gather from part of his study of the common snipe.

Castleberg Titles

How They Lived in the Yorkshire Dales	£8.99
Birds of the Lake District	£6.50
Birds of the Yorkshire Dales	£6.50
Ghost-hunting in the Yorkshire Dales	£5.99
Music of the Yorkshire Dales	£5.99
Cuckoo Town – Dales Life in the 1950's	£6.50
Sacred Places of the Lake District	£6.50
Beatrix Potter – Her Life in the Lake District	£6.20
The Lost Village of Mardale	£5.60
One Hundred Tales of the Settle-Carlisle Railway	£6.99
The Story of Ribblehead Viaduct	£5.50
How They Built the Settle-Carlisle Railway	£5.50
Garsdale – History of a Junction Station	£6.50
Mile by Mile on the Settle to Carlisle	£5.99
The Men Who Made the Settle to Carlisle	£5.99
How They Lived in Old Settle	£5.50
Life in the Lancashire Milltowns	£5.99
Watch the Birdie	£7.99
Nobbut Middlin'	£6.99
Nowt's Same	£6.50
You're Only Old Once	£5.99

Mini biographies:	Edward Elgar in the Yorkshire Dales	£4.99
	Fred Taylor – Yorkshire Cheesemaker	£4.99
	Tot Lord and the Bone Caves	£4.50
	Edith Carr – Life on Malham Moor	£4.50

Orders to **Kingfisher Productions**, 'Felmersham', Mills Road,
Osmington Mills, Weymouth, Dorset DT3 6HE
Tel & Fax 01305 832906   www.railwayvideo.com

All post free in the UK. £2.50 per item overseas.
Please allow 28 days for delivery, although we do endeavour to send
on the day of receiving the order.